Industry & Analysis' (I&A) staff of industry, trade and economic analysts devise and implement international trade, investment, and export promotion strategies that strengthen the global competitiveness of U.S. industries. These initiatives unlock export, and investment opportunities for U.S. businesses by combining in-depth quantitative and qualitative analysis with ITA's industry relationships.

For more information, visit
www.trade.gov/industry

I&A is part of the International Trade Administration, whose mission is to create prosperity by strengthening the competitiveness of U.S. industry, promoting trade and investment, and ensuring fair trade and compliance with trade laws and agreements.

INTERNATIONAL
TRADE
ADMINISTRATION

Gerry Zapiain, Senior International Trade Specialist in the Office of Health and Information Technologies, served as the lead author of this report. Special thanks to **Julian Richards** of the Office of Trade and Economic Analysis, who calculated the precise market rankings.

Considerable credit is due to **ITA's Global Healthcare Technologies Team** led by **Tembi Secrist** for their immeasurable contributions to this study. Thanks to **Anette Salama, Hiroyuki Hanawa, Connie Irrera, Monique Roos, Alicia Herrera, Maher Siblini, Tracy Yeoh, and Chamberlain Eke** for constituting a world-class team.

Finally, the author owes an extraordinary note of thanks to **Rebecca Gudicello**, Senior Advisor to the Assistant Secretary for Industry and Analysis, and to **Jennifer Boger**, Health Industries Team Leader, for their insightful reviews and comments on countless drafts.

Table of Contents

This Page Intentionally Left Blank

Executive Summary

U.S. medical device companies are highly regarded globally for their innovations and high-technology products. Investment in medical device research and development more than doubled in recent decades, and research and development investment in the domestic sector remains more than twice the average for all U.S. manufacturers.

The global medical devices market offers tremendous opportunity for U.S. manufacturers, as well as significant challenges, for government policymakers seeking to support U.S. export competitiveness in overseas markets. Creating new and sustained export opportunities for U.S. companies will require a concerted effort to remove or diminish market access barriers, helping U.S. firms to capture a larger share of the world import market. Encouraging and fostering U.S.-based healthcare industries is critical to the future of the U.S. economy, which is why medical technology is a National Export Initiative priority. The U.S. government, through several agencies and in particular through ITA, pursues a multi-prong effort for the benefit of U.S. exporters consisting of market research, policy analysis and formulation, and on-the-ground vetting of potential partners.

Besides the steady growth seen in the largest and more mature medical device markets that is likely to continue into the future, there are other promising markets for these products in Southeast Asia and Latin America. Through bilateral and multilateral fora, the U.S. government stands ready to help the medical device sector further develop and enhance its global competitiveness and make a meaningful contribution towards improving individual and public health worldwide.

This *Top Markets Report* examines 84 different markets in terms of U.S. export history, forecasted market risk and rewards for exporters of medical technology; *per capita* spending in markets; and market size. As U.S. exports of medical technology tend to be on the cutting edge of sophistication and advancement, data were used to highlight those markets that would likely be willing and able to make the necessary outlays for acquisition of more costly therapies. Furthermore, as medical technology unfolds and crosses new technological boundaries, innovative and developed regulatory systems are necessary to keep pace and ensure public health. The existence of a developed and internationally-harmonized regulatory agency is seen as important to U.S. exporters of medical technology and was a part of this ranking.

This Page Intentionally Left Blank

Overview and Key Findings

Introduction

The global medical devices market offers tremendous opportunity for U.S. manufacturers, as well as significant challenges, for government policymakers seeking to support U.S. export competitiveness in overseas markets. Creating new and sustained export opportunities for U.S. companies will require a concerted effort to remove or diminish market access barriers, helping U.S. firms to capture a larger share of the world import market. Encouraging and fostering U.S.-based healthcare industries is critical to the future of the U.S. economy, which is why medical technology is a National Export Initiative priority.

Despite uncertain economic conditions in key markets around the world, large and small players in the U.S. medical device industry show adaptability and tenacity, and companies are optimistic about the future. Medical device companies have found new opportunities for development in the face of uneven international economic growth and continually-changing regulatory systems.

Top Markets: Key Findings and Methodology

This *Top Markets Report* examines 84 different markets in terms of U.S. export history, forecasted market risk and rewards for exporters of medical technology; *per capita* spending in markets; and market size.

Methodology

This report uses a widely accepted definition of medical devices, similar to that used by the World Health Organization (WHO) and the United States Food and Drug Administration (FDA). A medical device is defined as any piece of equipment or apparatus used to treat or diagnose an illness and comes into direct contact with the patient. Pharmaceuticals and laboratory equipment are not within the scope of this report.

International industry information and market profiles have been provided by the International Trade Administration's (ITA) Global Health Team. ITA's Global Health Team, consisting of international trade experts at United States Embassies and Consulates worldwide, as well as in all fifty states, and industry experts in Washington, D.C., is dedicated to enhancing the global competitiveness of the U.S. health industry, expanding its market access and increasing exports. It accomplishes this through in-depth research and a variety of resources and services for U.S. companies, such as seminars, webinars and Gold Key and Platinum Key Services. Relevant data were collected by surveying international posts with the template questionnaire found at Appendix 2.

Data for current and forecast sales values of medical devices are sourced from statistics collected by the Census Bureau, the International Trade Commission (ITC) and Business Monitor International (BMI).

Market size and forecasts have been estimated using a trade-based approach, as most countries are reliant on imports. Estimates have been derived by looking at imports while considering domestic production, including exports. For practical purposes, we define a generally-accepted range of HTS codes as the entire market.[1] HTS codes are used for export forecast calculations in this report as they most accurately encompass international trade in medical devices. This report uses trade data through the end of 2015.

Projections were based upon the current estimate size and conditions, considering factors such as expected need, propensity of lifestyle disease, proposed spending, regulatory developments and other social factors, such as international health projects, economic performance, trends in import levels, size and performance of domestic manufacturing sector, national healthcare development plans and currency issues.

Figure 1: Near-Term Medical Device Export Market Rankings				
1. Germany	5. Belgium	9. France	13. Norway	17. Denmark
2. Japan	6. Switzerland	10. Australia	14. Sweden	18. Singapore
3. Netherlands	7. United Kingdom	11. Mexico	15. Italy	19. Ireland
4. Canada	8. China	12. Austria	16. Korea	20. Israel

Because of remarkable advances in science and technology, including those in the health care industry, life expectancy in many countries has been steadily growing. As a result, the expanding proportion of elderly people promises further growth of demand for medical devices. The total combined quantitative rankings reflect the degree to which they are existent in each market; aging populations in developing economies now tend to expect therapies for health conditions that previous generations simply endured or that were life-ending.

Aging populations worldwide, coupled with extended life expectancy, create a sustainable demand for medical devices. As elderly populations' healthcare is frequently government-subsidized in markets around the world, home healthcare is also becoming of increased importance, as related technologies become more effective, and healthcare budgets are more closely scrutinized.

Industry Overview and Competitiveness

U.S. medical device companies are highly regarded globally for their innovations and high-technology products. Investment in medical device research and development more than doubled in recent decades, and research and development investment in the domestic sector remains more than twice the average for all U.S. manufacturers.

The United States is expected to continue to play a leading role in medical device research and development. After declining in 2009, research and development spending rebounded to $2.9 billion in 2010 and $7.3 billion in 2011. From 2013 to 2020, larger medical device companies are expected to increase their research and development budgets by approximately 3 percent, while the rest of the industry is expected to increase spending for this element by more than 5 percent.[2]

The U.S. medical device industry is highly diversified and produces a variety of products to diagnose and treat patients, ranging from tongue depressors to complex programmable pacemakers. The United States medical devices industry is known for producing high quality products using advanced technology resulting from significant investment in research and development. During the last decade, the United States medical device industry experienced unprecedented advancement in

innovative and developed technologies, leading to the birth of new therapies and growth in overall healthcare industry.

The major U.S. medical device companies include: Baxter®, Beckman Coulter®, Becton Dickinson®, Boston Scientific®, GE Healthcare Technologies®, Johnson & Johnson®, Medtronic®, St. Jude® and Stryker Corporation®, to name a few. In addition, the following medical device industry trade associations closely follow the industry: Advanced Medical Technology Association (AdvaMed), Dental Trade Alliance (DTA), Medical Device Manufacturers Association (MDMA), Medical Imaging Technology Association (MITA) and the International Association of Medical Equipment Remarketers & Servicers (IAMERS).

Size and Shape of the U.S. Medical Devices Industry

For purposes of estimating of the size and shape of the U.S. medical devices industry, the U.S. Census Bureau (Census) uses the North American Industry Classification System (NAICS) codes in its five year Economic Census, which was most recently executed in 2012. Those NAICS codes used by Census for this estimation are as follows:

- 325413 *In-Vitro* Diagnostic Substances Manufacturing
- 334510 Electro-medical and Electrotherapeutic Apparatus Manufacturing
- 334517 Irradiation Apparatus Manufacturing
- 339112 Surgical and Medical Instrument Manufacturing
- 339113 Surgical Appliances and Supplies Manufacturing
- 339114 Dental Equipment and Supplies Manufacturing
- 339115 Ophthalmic Goods Manufacturing

- *In-vitro* diagnostic substances (NAICS 325413) account for about 14 percent of value of shipment (VOS) of total exports and includes chemical, biological or radioactive substances used for diagnostic tests performed in test tubes, Petri dishes, machines and other diagnostic test-type devices.

- Electro-medical equipment (NAICS 334510) represents the third largest subsector (17 percent of VOS) and accounts for a variety of powered devices, including pacemakers, patient-monitoring systems, MRI machines, diagnostic imaging equipment (including informatics equipment) and ultrasonic scanning devices.

- Irradiation apparatus (NAICS 334517); about 8 percent of VOS) includes X-ray devices and other diagnostic imaging as well as computed tomography equipment (CT).

- Surgical and medical instruments (NAICS 339112) comprises the largest subgroup (about 29 percent of VOS) of the U.S. medical device industry. The category includes anesthesia apparatus, orthopedic instruments, optical diagnostic apparatus, blood transfusion devices, syringes, hypodermic needles and catheters.

- Surgical appliances and supplies (NAICS 339113) is the second largest U.S. medical device subsector with about 22 percent of the total measured by VOS. The category covers a wide range of products, including artificial joints and limbs, stents, orthopedic appliances, surgical dressings, disposable surgical drapes, hydrotherapy appliances, surgical kits, rubber medical and surgical gloves, and wheelchairs.

- Dental equipment and supplies (NAIC 339114; 3 percent of VOS) consists of equipment, instruments and supplies used by dentists, dental hygienists and laboratories. Specific products include dental hand instruments, plaster, drills, amalgams, cements, sterilizers and dental chairs.

- Ophthalmic goods (NAIC 339115; 6 percent of VOS) includes eyeglass frames, lenses and related optical and magnification products.

In 2015, the total value of U.S. industry shipments for the products covered by the NAICS categories identified above was worth $43 billion and, in recent years, has experienced approximately 1.5 percent annual growth. Median medical technology jobs paid 15 percent more than the average U.S. manufacturing job. In the 2012 Economic Census, it was reported that the medical device industry employed more than 356,000 people in the United States, at over 5,800 establishments, earning an average wage between $60,000 and $70,000. Most

Generally accepted WHO definition of medical device and medical equipment:

Medical device (brief): An article, instrument, apparatus or machine that is used in the prevention, diagnosis or treatment of illness or disease, or for detecting, measuring, restoring, correcting or modifying the structure or function of the body for some health purpose. Typically, the purpose of a medical device is not achieved by pharmacological, immunological or metabolic means.

Medical equipment: Medical devices requiring calibration, maintenance, repair, user training and decommissioning – activities usually managed by clinical engineers. Medical equipment is used for the specific purposes of diagnosis and treatment of disease or rehabilitation following disease or injury; it can be used alone or in combination with any accessory, consumable or other piece of medical equipment. Medical equipment excludes implantable, disposable or single-use medical devices.

of these companies are small and medium-sized enterprises (SMEs): 80 percent of these are estimated to have fewer than 50 employees, and many (notably innovative start-up companies) have little or no sales revenue. Taken together, these companies set up an explosively competitive industry profile flourishing on innovation. Larger players in this field carefully consider partnerships with their smaller counterparts and often enter into mergers or acquisition deals to increase their product lines and offer economies of scale resulting in more value-focused healthcare solutions.

Medical device companies are located throughout the country but are mainly concentrated in certain regions known for other high-technology industries, such as microelectronics and biotechnology. The states with the highest number of medical device companies include California, Florida, New York, Pennsylvania, Michigan, Massachusetts, Illinois, Minnesota and Georgia.
The United States also holds a competitive advantage in several industries upon which the medical device industry relies, including

microelectronics, telecommunications, instrumentation, biotechnology and software development. Collaborations have led to recent advances, including health information technology ("Health IT"), neuro-stimulators, stent technologies, biomarkers, robotic assistance and implantable electronic devices. Certain areas of patient care and treatment have developed remarkably, and advancements in mobile applications and devices, such as health monitoring devices developed at one time for the U.S space program, have been modified and made practical for a widening number of patients. Health IT promises to have vast market potential, as it develops in a multitude of forms. Communications companies are progressively becoming players in this field, developing telemedicine applications and monitoring systems. Because the medical technology industry is fueled by innovation and the ongoing quest for better ways of treating or diagnosing medical problems, the future growth of this sector remains positive. For more information on Health IT, please see the related Top Markets Report at www.trade.gov/topmarkets.

The United States is home to 141 accredited medical schools and approximately 400 major teaching hospitals and health systems, many of which rank among the best in the world. Many of these academic institutions collaborate with medical device companies to develop new medical technologies.[3]

The Made in America Movement (MAM) stated in 2015 that the United States has become an increasingly attractive location for business investment from global countries. According to AT Kearney's 2013 FDI Confidence Index, the United States surged past countries like China, Brazil and India to become the country with the top foreign direct investment (FDI) prospects globally, as ranked by 32 companies representing 28 countries in multiple industry sectors. More companies are looking to locate to the United States after considering competitive advantages, such as skills and productivity, innovation, energy reserves and access to the largest consumer market in the world.[4]

Global Industry Landscape

Besides leading the world in the production of medical devices, the United States is the largest medical devices consumer. The United States

medical device market is valued at more than $140 billion in 2015, which accounts for approximately 45 percent of the global market according to the U.S. Government Accountability Office's (GAO) 2014 statistics. U.S. exports of medical devices were valued at approximately $45 billion in 2015, and imports were valued at $54 billion.

Over the past decade the value of imported medical devices has steadily increased, gradually eroding the previous trade surplus. The majority of imports are lower-tech products, such as surgical gloves and instruments. Continuing shifts in trade patterns have resulted in China and Mexico becoming significant exporters of mid to lower-tech equipment and supplies to the United States.

The surgical and medical instruments category (NAICS 339112) represents the subgroup with the most activity in the United States medical device sector. This category includes numerous price-sensitive lower-technology devices which can be more easily substituted with higher technology medical device products. While exports of surgical and medical instruments grew by 27.5 percent from 2007 to 2012, imports grew by almost an identical rate.

Other NAICS product categories have also shown varying growth rates in both exports and imports between 2007 and 2012. For example, exports of surgical appliances and supplies (NAICS 339113) grew by 22.5 percent and imports by 26 percent; exports of ophthalmic goods (NAICS 339115) grew by 7.5 percent and imports by 33 percent.

The U.S. medical device industry is expected to remain highly competitive globally, partially because of national characteristics that facilitate bringing new and innovative technologies to market. The industry has increasingly embraced globalization, and an ever-growing number of multinational firms is aggressively pursuing markets around the world. These firms are focusing greater attention on international sales, joint ventures, mergers and acquisitions. Global demand for medical devices is driven by increasing expenditures and activities on health care by developing markets with the building of new hospitals and clinics, establishment of public health insurance and greater focus on health. In addition, global demand should continue to grow due to lifestyle diseases, aging populations in major markets, new and significant emerging markets and rising global income levels in developing countries. Further, global convergence of standards and regulatory requirements should help facilitate global market growth and trade opportunities.

Key Trends

Cost Efficiency

Increased competition, developed and cross-bred therapies, and cost containment have more keenly focused the medical device industry's attention on creating value for payers and patients rather than the traditional means of mining revenue by investing in research, development and innovation. Companies are looking toward holistic, coordinated therapies and healthcare solutions to shift to value-based healthcare, providing value with efficiency. By addressing therapies as an all-inclusive treatment package, medical device companies can better assist providers in delivering on their obligations to patients, controlling costs and simplifying transactions.

Export Market Mixture

As expected, the European Union (EU), Japan and Canada are extremely large and lucrative export markets for medical devices. These stable, mature markets, however, have relatively low (3 to 5 percent) annual growth rates. In order to facilitate expansion, medical device companies recognize that they must also look at developing countries for future growth. In some of these, demand for medical devices is growing at double digit growth in contrast to certain larger, slower growing markets in more developed countries. Significant yet underserved populations in developing markets often grow steadily, face similar aging populations and increasing lifestyle diseases and have an increased awareness of health technology development. Furthermore, many markets deemed as "developing" have highly urbanized population centers with rising expendable wealth, making certain sectors of markets interesting to exporters. A U.S. exporter would be best served by investigating both larger developed markets as well as emerging, raw markets in order to find the best export effectiveness.

Regulatory Convergence

For the medical device industry to fully realize its potential in developing markets, standards for regulatory approval, risk management and quality must improve and continue along the path of international convergence to meet global standards. To that end, the Global Harmonization Task Force (GHTF), formed as a voluntary organization comprised of regulators and industry with five founding members consisting of the United States, Canada, Japan, the European Union and Australia, had as its core objective streamlining and harmonizing regulatory standards. Developing countries like India, China, Mexico and Brazil benefited in the work of GHTF by considering that organization's guidance documents while designing their own regulatory systems.

In October 2011, representatives from the medical device regulatory authorities of Australia, Brazil, Canada, China, EU, Japan and the United States, as

Figure 2: Trade flows by NAICS for Medical Devices Sector				
NAICS Code/Description	2014 Exports (USD Billions)	2015 Exports (USD Billions)	2014 Imports (USD Billions)	2015 Imports (USD Billions)
325413 – *In Vitro* Diagnostic Substance	$6.0	$6.1	$3.3	$3.5
334510 – Electro-medical Apparatus	$8.3	$7.5	$10.4	$10.3
334517 - Irradiation Apparatus	$3.4	$3.6	$3.8	$3.7
339112 - Surgical and Medical Instruments	$12.6	$12.4	$11.3	$12.3
339113 - Surgical Appliances and Supplies	$9.3	$9.6	$12.9	$13.7
339114 - Dental Equipment and Supplies	$1.2	$1.2	$1.2	$1.3
339115 - Ophthalmic Goods	$2.7	$2.7	$5.1	$5.1
Total	$43.5	$43.2	$47.9	$49.9

well as the WHO, met in Ottawa, Ontario, Canada to address the establishment and operation of a new vehicle to further expand the work of the GHTF. The new organization, the International Medical Device Regulators Forum (IMDRF), is a voluntary group of medical device regulators from around the world who have come together to build on the strong foundational work of the GHTF. IMDRF aims to accelerate international medical device regulatory harmonization and convergence. The enhanced participation of developing countries' medical device regulatory agencies in IMDRF activities coupled with guidance issued by GHTF will be critical in establishing regulatory regimes for medical devices that are distinct from traditional pharmaceuticals. Upon further development in this area, the medical device industry will continue to evolve as a global industry and better direct its energies to the development of even more innovative, life-improving and life-saving medical technologies.

Challenges, Barriers and Opportunities

The U.S. industry primarily faces competition from Germany (Siemens® and Braun®), Japan (Hitachi® , Medical Corporation® and Toshiba®) and the Netherlands (Philips Electronics®), in high-technology products. Notably, as a result of its acquisition policy, Philips currently produces more medical devices in the United States than in Europe. It is important to note that most of these foreign companies manufacture significant amounts of medical devices (or components) in the United States. High quality but lower technology medical device firms are being challenged by numerous lower-cost producers from China, Brazil, Korea, Taiwan, Mexico and India, all of which are building up their domestic industries and beginning to compete globally. While the United States will likely retain its competitive edge for the foreseeable future, international markets are expected to remain competitive.

Key Export Policies

Opportunities for expansion of U.S. medical device exports will come from certain key ongoing policy and activities. With respect to accessing developing countries, the contributions of IMDRF will play a significant role in the international convergence of regulatory requirements that can lead to greater

market penetration. In addition, continued focus on reducing or eliminating tariffs in key markets and higher reimbursement rates will also significantly influence growth. Further, assisting SMEs in export opportunities through market information, trade missions and other trade promotion activities can also increase overall U.S. exports for this industry.

The U.S. medical device industry needs and expects the U.S. government to remain involved in the several following areas that will establish and improve trade conditions:

- negotiate strongly to reduce or eliminate tariffs on medical devices
- address foreign governments' regulatory policies that are inconsistent with international regulatory convergence efforts and that may cause unfair discrimination against U.S. industry
- educate the industry on how to comply with foreign regulatory requirements
- provide export assistance opportunities similar to what foreign governments provide for their industries

U.S. medical device exports will need to understand what export requirements exist for their products. The rules that U.S. companies must follow when exporting medical devices depend on whether their devices have been cleared by the U.S. Food and Drug Administration (FDA). Medical devices that are legally marketed in the United States may be exported anywhere in the world without prior FDA notification or approval. Devices that have not been approved or cleared in the United States must follow the export provisions of the Federal Food, Drug and Cosmetic (FD&C) Act.

Firms exporting products from the United States are often asked by foreign customers or foreign governments to supply proof of the products' statuses as regulated by the FDA. An export certificate is a document prepared by FDA that has information about a product's regulatory or marketing status in the United States. A Certificate to Foreign Government (CFG) is the most frequently requested type of export certificate, but a Certificate of Exportability may also be requested when exporting devices under sections 801(e)(1) and 802 of the FD&C Act or when exporting Non-Clinical Research-Use-Only devices.

Depending on the medical device, there are three possible sections of the FD&C Act that may be applicable, each with different requirements, if these have not been approved for sale in the United States.

Section 801(e)(1) of the FD&C Act governs the rules for exporting non-cleared Class I or Class II devices, not including Class II devices subject to performance standards.

Section 802 covers exporting non-cleared Class II devices subject to performance standards, unapproved Class III devices, devices for investigational use, devices intended for further processing and devices intended for treatment of diseases not prevalent in the United States.

Section 801(e)(2) governs export of non-cleared Class III investigational devices, banned devices, devices for which a premarket authorization (PMA) has not been approved as well as other devices which do not meet requirements of Section 802.

For more information on FDA export requirements for medical devices, please visit http://www.fda.gov/MedicalDevices/DeviceRegulationandGuidance/ImportingandExportingDevices/ExportingMedicalDevices/default.htm.

Export Barriers

Regulatory and reimbursement requirements for medical devices vary from country to country, creating complications for U.S. exporters. Certain countries, including India, some Latin American countries and parts of Asia, still maintain high tariffs on some medical products, reducing the net sale price of medical devices. U.S. firms also face increasing competition globally, especially from foreign firms that can successfully compete on the basis of price. U.S. firms without sufficient resources to conduct necessary market research are especially vulnerable.

- *International Regulatory Environments*: The medical device industry is highly regulated, and regulatory environments in the United States and abroad have serious implications on industry performance. An increasingly common practice among developing countries is the establishment of national regulatory srequirements above and beyond the requirements of developed countries. Device firms tend to devote tremendous amounts of time and money to determine such requirements, conduct additional clinical trials and pay additional user fees. These national requirements may sometimes be established to protect the domestic industry, to be a source of revenue for the government or both.

- *International Reimbursement Payment Environments*: Reimbursement or payment practices in certain countries have also had negative impacts on the U.S. industry. Many countries around the world are facing the same intensifying costs of health care as the United States and are trying to address costs by reducing reimbursement rates, establishing price caps, requiring mandatory price reductions, using diagnostic related groups (DRGs), limiting funds available for medical device purchases and/or requiring inappropriate information about the product or pricing data from the manufacturer. Germany, France, Japan, Taiwan, Korea, China and Brazil are all examples of major markets where industry has reported that prices for medical devices and reimbursement rates have been potentially set lower than the value of the technology, thus limiting the introduction of advanced technologies and making it difficult for U.S. firms to be profitable in these markets. Most medical devices have a life-cycle of 18 to 24 months, which makes reimbursement key for continued product innovation, including incremental improvements. The U.S. government has encouraged foreign governments to take the overall value of advanced technologies and other costs in healthcare delivery into greater consideration when establishing their reimbursement rates.

- *Regulatory Convergence Efforts*: Convergence of medical device regulations is one way to reduce the industry's burden and ensure maximum accessibility of safe, effective medical devices by patients. U.S. industry would like to see products "approved once, accepted everywhere." ITA is encouraging foreign governments to make use of guidance documents produced by international bodies, most notably IMDRF, to encourage regulatory convergence and to eliminate or reduce redundant and unnecessary regulatory procedures.

- *IPR and Counterfeit Medical Devices*: Although intellectual property rights (IPR) and counterfeiting have not posed as significant a problem for medical device firms as they have in the pharmaceutical industry, the sector is beginning to face related revenue losses with increasing frequency. IPR violations include using medical device firms' patented technology to manufacture a competing medical device or unauthorized use of a registered trademark. Similarly, counterfeit medical devices are copies of patented medical devices that are manufactured and marketed without following the requisite approval process, which can result in unsafe products on the market. IPR violations occur in markets that may not fully respect or enforce patent protection, such as China. There is limited data on counterfeit medical devices, but based on feedback from industry, the most frequent incidences are in IVD reagents and solutions, contact lenses, medical test kits, combination products and components parts, such as semiconductors used in imaging equipment. U.S. industry loses market share to counterfeit products, and patients are subject to unnecessary risks. ITA, and other USG agencies like PTO and USTR, is actively engaged in global, regional and bilateral dialogues to address this problem.

- *SMEs' Lack of Resources*: The majority of the U.S. medical device industry consists of small and medium-sized firms that reinvest much of their revenue into research and development to make incremental improvements to their technology. A majority of these companies do not have the resources to conduct sophisticated export market research. In addition, many smaller companies are so focused on entering the U.S. market first that they put off exporting

until they have become profitable in the United States. The domestic market, however, can be more difficult to enter than some foreign markets due to stringent FDA regulations and complex reimbursement policies with Medicare and Medicaid.

Opportunities

U.S. medical device exporters have and will continue to benefit from international trade agreements, such as NAFTA and TPP.

In 1994, the North American Free Trade Agreement between the United States, Canada and Mexico (NAFTA) entered into force, ultimately eliminating duties and quantitative restrictions for trade in medical devices. NAFTA created the world's largest free trade area to date, which now links 474 million people and produces roughly $20.5 trillion worth of goods and services.

Trade between the United States and its NAFTA partners has soared since the agreement entered into force: U.S. goods exports to the NAFTA partners have increased by 289 percent from 1993 to 2014 from $142 billion to $552 billion. U.S. two-way goods trade with Canada and Mexico exceeds U.S. goods trade with the European Union and Japan combined. Annual exports of U.S. medical devices to Canada have more than tripled since the year before NAFTA was signed into law, and exports of the same to Mexico have more than quadrupled.

The Trans-Pacific Partnership agreement (TPP) is a trade agreement covering eleven U.S. trading partners: Australia, Brunei, Canada, Chile, Japan, Malaysia, Mexico, New Zealand, Peru, Singapore and Vietnam. It is dedicated to increasing the trade of goods and services between member states. TPP goes beyond NAFTA in many important ways, effectively updating trade relations between the partners and setting new, higher standards for U.S.

Figure 3: Medical Devices Market: Forecast for Growth, in USD Billions					
Region	2016	2017	2018	2019	2020
Americas	166.6	176.5	187.3	197.9	208.6
Asia/Pacific	68.7	72.6	77.6	82.9	88.6
Central/Eastern	14.6	15.7	17	18.1	19.1
Middle East/Africa	10	10.8	11.5	12.5	13.2
Western Europe	79.5	85.1	92.6	101.4	106.2
Total	339.5	360.8	386.1	412.8	435.8

Source: Worldwide Medical Devices Forecast to 2020

regional trade agreements. The agreement also includes dispute resolution mechanisms as well as regulations relating to government procurement practices and intellectual property protections.

The agreement removes tariffs on medical devices, supports increased regulatory coherence among the member states and widens stakeholder influence and transparency with respect to reimbursement and pricing. Ultimately, the TPP will result in quicker approvals of medical devices, benefiting U.S. companies that export to signatory partner countries. For more information on the benefits of the TPP including for the medical device industry, please visit www.trade.gov/tpp.

3D Medical Printing

3D medical printing is expected to develop and find its niche in several areas of medicine. U.S. universities and research hospital groups work with U.S. manufacturers to discover opportunities and meet challenges in this new field, including investigating applications for 3D printing of biomaterials and living cells; adapting 3D printing for surgical planning; and developing applications for tumor removal, spinal surgery and cranio-fallacial surgery and reconstruction.

A 3D printer "prints" in three dimensions, in layers, with each successive level of the substrate approximating the final product. The first 3D printers were developed in the 1980s in the United States and were used by car and airplane manufacturers to design specialized parts on a computer and then create prototypes for analysis. The medical device industry is finding applications for this technology, with custom-designed hearing aids, dental and other implantables, prosthetics and other devices that can be modified to best serve the user. Application of customized 3D printed implants reduces surgical complications and promotes patient compatibility.

The cost of producing 3D custom devices has limited the development of the science, but as the technology advances, overall costs should decline, making customized devices more accessible. The FDA is investigating how to regulate 3D printing of medical devices and is expected to release a guidance document this year. The European Commission has received requests to consider 3D printing regulations in its current review of the Medical Devices Directive (MDD). Interest in 3D medical printing is not limited to the United States and Europe and promises to remain at the cutting edge of personalized medicine.

This Page Intentionally Left Blank

Country Case Studies

The following pages include country case studies that summarize U.S. medical device export opportunities in selected markets. The overviews outline ITA's analysis of the U.S. export potential in each market and offer recommendations to exporters that can improve their competitiveness. The markets represent a range of countries to illustrate a variety of points – and not the top markets overall.

This Page Intentionally Left Blank

Germany

Germany has a long history of producing high quality medical equipment, with a particular emphasis on diagnostic imaging, dental products and optical technologies. Not only is Germany the third largest market in the world after the United States and Japan but is also by far the largest European market, twice the size of the French market and three times as large as those of Italy, the United Kingdom and Spain.

Overall Rank

1

Germany has a strong healthcare system in terms of infrastructure, hospital beds and trained staff. There are 500,671 beds in 1,996 hospitals (around 596 public hospitals, 706 non-profit and 694 private hospitals), 2,000 medical supply stores, 1,187 rehabilitation centers, 21,062 pharmacies and 150,000 doctors' offices. Well-established infrastructure makes the healthcare industry the largest employer in Germany with currently 6.2 million employees. Another 4 million jobs depend on the healthcare sector. One out of five jobs in Germany is linked to the healthcare sector.

Accordingly, German healthcare expenditures are comparatively high but also increasingly cost-contained. In 2013, total expenditures increased 4 percent to EUR 314.9 billion, roughly 11.2 percent of GDP. In *per capita* terms, expenditure is estimated at EUR 3,910, exceeded only by Denmark, the United States, Switzerland and Norway.

Approximately 76.8 percent of healthcare spending is sourced from the public sector, mostly from statutory health insurances. As public health insurance funds continue to record deficits averaging

EUR 3.3 billion and public hospitals operate at a loss, health reforms and cost-cutting measures keep the market tight with increased pressure on prices. Hospitals in the public sector are pressed to maintain existing equipment rather than investing in new units. Private hospitals, now at 30 percent of total hospitals in Germany, as well as the more than 60 university hospitals with specialized departments, seek price-competitive, state-of-the-art technologies and equipment offering proven cost savings.

Country Highlights
Capital: Berlin
Population: 83.8 million (2013)
GDP: $3.4 trillion (2013)
Currency: Euro (EUR/€)
Language: German
Contact: Anette Salama, Senior Commercial Specialist
anette.salama@trade.gov
+49-211-737767-60

Taking into account the heightened scrutiny on spending within certain sectors, the German healthcare industry offers high growth potential and provides opportunities for U.S. medical technology exports. The Federal Ministry of Economics anticipates that by 2030, an additional 2 million people will be employed in the healthcare industry. Current austerity measures are likely to hit the pharmaceutical industry harder than the medical device industry, which continues to be a job engine and is expected to achieve steady growth over the next five years with annual growth rates of 3 to 4 percent. In 2012, over 51 percent of German healthcare technology manufacturers reported to have created new jobs with a very positive outlook for future growth.

According to the German Advanced Medical Technology Association (BVMed), the medical devices industry employed 195,000 persons with a market valued at EUR 25.19 billion in 2014. The German market accounts for 40 percent of the entire EU market for medical devices.

For general statistical information published by the German Federal Statistics Office, please visit *destatis.de/EN*.

Market Entry

<u>Distribution Practices</u>

Most medical equipment imported into Germany is either sold directly through a local subsidiary with a field sales force, through medical distributors with an established distribution network or through appointed agents or manufacturer representatives. Local representation or market presence is essential when considering differing standards and certifications, warehousing costs, maintenance, accessibility and local marketing/sales preferences/discussions. An agreement for a representative party or agent is often a cost effective mechanism to enter the market, but under German law—even if the agent's performance is not satisfactory—it can be difficult and costly to terminate the agreement, particularly under an exclusive arrangement. A representation or distributorship agreement may be harder to arrange, but the German associate will generally purchase the product which is to be sold, thus sharing the marketing risk. Finding a mid-size distributor covering all of the German, or German-speaking, market has become more difficult because large manufacturers have increasingly acquired experienced distributors to gain access to established distribution channels rather than developing those themselves. For example, GE Healthcare has acquired Medicalis and Idel, and Donjoy has acquired Ormed, among others. As Germany's healthcare market is decentralized and regional, it may therefore be a viable alternative to seek regionally active and well-established dealers or distributors for northern, southern and eastern Germany with defined territories.

In addition to complying with standards, U.S. companies must meet additional criteria to assure product acceptance recognition and marketability when trying to enter the German market. For example, product information and technical data sheets must be provided in German.

Companies should also provide operation and instruction manuals in German to ensure proper understanding and usage of equipment, as well as provide reliable after-sales servicing and product support or select qualified agents or distributors who are capable of providing quality service. U.S. companies should maintain close contact and good feedback with agents and dealer/distributors in Germany in order to stay informed about market developments, trade issues, regulations and laws concerning their products.

<u>Product Standards</u>

The German market for medical devices is regulated by German and EU directives, standards and safety regulations. The requirements are complex and based on environmental, consumer health, safety and social concerns. Not all standards are mandatory, but compliance greatly enhances a product's marketability. Advice on the requirements and compliance certification in the case of a specific product should be sought from the below referenced sources.

The German Medical Devices Act (MPG) of 1994 was amended in August 2015. It applies to all equipment, instruments, devices and materials used on or in the human body and is applicable when seeking approval for a device to enter the German market. Exceptions include those devices that achieve their intended effect pharmacologically. About 400,000 different medical products fall under this legislation. The MPG implements EU directives covering medical and diagnostic products. Devices complying with the MPG or its equivalent laws in other EU countries must carry CE Marking. Devices with CE Marking have the advantage of being permitted on the market anywhere in the EU without further certification requirements.

<u>Packaging and Labeling</u>

The European Union does not set packaging and labeling requirements in general, only setting them in very specific high-risk product related cases. In the absence of any EU-wide rules, the exporter has to consult national rules or inquire about voluntary agreements among forwarders, which affect packaging and labeling of containers and outer packaging. The importer or freight forwarder is the first point of contact for shipping documents and outer packaging/labeling. EU customs legislation only regulates administrative procedures, such as type of certificate and the mention of rule of origin on the customs forms and shipping documents.

Payment and Financing Practices

In Germany, the period allowed for payment is between 30 and 60 days. Early payments are often credited with a 3 percent discount, and supplier credits in the form of LoCs are common.

Practices regarding financing, availability of capital and payment schedules are comparable to those in the United States. There are no restrictions or barriers on the movement of capital, foreign exchange earnings or dividends. Most major U.S. banks are represented in Frankfurt, the country's financial hub. Similarly, a large number of German banks, including some of the partially state-owned regional banks, maintain subsidiaries, branches and/or branch offices in the United States. Germany is not eligible for support from OPIC, TDA or similar agencies.

Tariffs and Import Regulation

There is no import duty on medical devices; a 19 percent import turnover tax is payable at the port entry. For customs clearance, a product description is required describing the use, origin and value of the product. The cost of the import-turnover tax is usually offset by ultimately passing it on to the end-user in later distribution stages in the form of a Value-Added Tax (VAT), which is known in Germany as Mehrwertsteuer (MwSt).

Current Market Trends

The current German government has proposed several new health plans to improve and ensure the quality of hospitals and doctor offices and provide the best healthcare to patients of any age group. As of January 2015, it is mandatory for each insured person to have an electronic health card, which stores personal patient data. The new Care Provision Strengthening Act (Versorgungsstärkungsgesetz) creates incentives for doctors to open their offices in rural areas due to a demographic aging among medical staff and resulting shutdowns of general practitioners' offices. In addition, the Hospital Structuring Act (Krankenhausstrukturgesetz) stipulates quality standards for hospitals and their review and screening. Large scale cost savings and further hospital efficiencies and consolidation are expected as a result.

Main Competitors

The German market for medical devices is sophisticated and well-served. Germany has a handful of large producers, headed by Siemens, B. Braun and Fresenius. Ninety-five percent of the German medical technology industry is characterized by small and mid-sized (SME) companies or sub-groups of larger companies. Almost 1,200 SME companies employ over 125,000 people, and 11,300 smaller companies employ around 75,000 people. Ninety-five percent of all companies employ less than 250 employees, and rarely does one company represent more than 2 percent of the entire sector. In addition, foreign industry giants such as Philips® (Netherlands), Hitachi® (Japan) and Toshiba® (Japan) are well entrenched in the market. GE Healthcare Technologies®, Medtronic®, Agilent®, 3M Healthcare®, Hollister®, Johnson & Johnson® and Medline® are only a few of the many German subsidiaries of U.S. medical device suppliers.

As a developed market, the German medical technology industry relies on export markets for continued growth. On average, German medical technology companies export between 60 percent and 65 percent of their products. In 2014, foreign sales rose by 2 percent, and the exports reached 68 percent of local production. Around one-fifth of these exports went to the United States. Next to this strong German manufacturing base, imports supply around three-quarters of the German medical market ($16.7 billion). Between 2007 and 2011 medical device imports recorded a CAGR of 6.6 percent in Euro terms and 7.0 percent in dollar terms. U.S. medical device exporters to Germany continue to hold a 27 to 30 percent import market share, depending on the product. U.S. suppliers of innovative and price-competitive products especially can compete strongly on the German market.

Current Demand

There is a stable demand for high quality advanced diagnostic and therapeutic equipment, innovative technologies and minimally invasive equipment in vascular surgery, urology, gastroenterology, dermatology and neuro-surgery. Major trends are wearable and wireless medical technologies. At the same time, the demand for specialized software to protect wireless medical devices and healthcare systems against cybercrime and malware is expected to increase. Furthermore, the German medical market experiences a clear trend toward personalized medicine based on individual patient requirements. This reflects on medical packaging with increased demand for flexible and compact packaging machines.

The trend is toward miniaturization of electro-medical equipment and nanotechnology products. New technologies in emergency and first responder care along with computer-assisted surgery are widely discussed among the German medical community. Germany is also proactive in coming up with solutions to address the aging population; therefore, there will be an uptick in demand for diagnostic equipment to detect chronic diseases in their early stages in order to prevent higher costs. It will also spur the demand for specialized wound care and easy-to-use homecare products for diabetes, orthopedic appliances and dialysis equipment. Third, big data technology is in high demand in all segments and in the context of evaluating data for new therapies and cost-containment measures as well as healthcare prevention.

Registration Process

The EU Commission, appointed in November 2014, is expected to consider a fundamental revision of the regulatory framework for medical devices after 2018 or 2019.

CE Marking is a legal requirement for a wide range of equipment manufacturers in Germany. CE Marking signifies that a product fulfills all necessary EU regulatory requirements. Certification requirements for use of CE Marking vary depending on the product. For some, such as those in the MPG low risk class I, the manufacturers (or importer/ authorized representative, if the product is manufactured outside the EU) may self-certify compliance with EU requirements and affix the mark. For others the certification of a "notified body" (an accredited certification agency such as TUV) will be required. For the medical aids sector, the workability and safety of a product is now considered satisfied by CE Marking. CE Marking is a visible indication that the manufacturer signed a "Declaration of Conformity" that requires it to perform all assessment testing prior to affixing the symbol, claiming compliance with all relevant CE Marking directives in force.

All electro-medical equipment in Germany must be suitable for use with 220 Volt, 50 cycle electrical current and should have VDE or TUEV approval. A UL approval is not a substitute but is helpful to obtain "GS/VDE," or GS/TUEV" approval in Germany. "GS" stands for "gepruefte Sicherheit" (safety tested). Although "GS" and the "VDE" (or "GS and TUV") marks are not required by law, they are highly recommended for marketing electro-medical goods in Germany.

The U.S. Product Safety Testing Institute, Underwriters Laboratories (UL), the VDE Testing and Certification Institute and TUV Product Service have formed a strategic alliance for testing of electromagnetic compatibility (EMC), which has resulted in the globally recognized EMC test mark. For manufacturers of electrical and electronic products, this cooperation has led to a substantial simplification of EMC testing. Through a single test carried out by one of these three partners, a product can now be awarded an international EMC mark, which replaces the national test marks in the major world markets of Europe, the United States and Japan.

Barriers

Companies exporting medical devices to Germany will not encounter any direct trade barriers or quotas. Non-tariff, indirect trade barriers could include the complex German reimbursement system or the need for additional registration procedures, for example, in the case of medical assistive technologies or products sold in pharmacies, with the requirement to apply for HMV or PZN codes, respectively. For Class 2 medical products, the German medical products law requires manufacturing and distribution control/quality control documentation.

Trade Events

BIOTECHNICA
October • Hanover, Germany • **biotechnica.de** Europe's leading trade fair for biotechnology, life sciences and laboratory equipment. More than 600 exhibitors.

REHACARE
September–October • Düsseldorf, Germany • **rehacare.de** Europe's premier rehabilitation and

care event. Open to the public. Approximately 50,000 visitors and 805 exhibitors from 32 countries.

A+A (Safety + Health at the Workplace)
October • Düsseldorf, Germany • **aplusa-online.de** The world's largest and most important specialist trade fair for all aspects of safety and security. Includes safety, security and health management, including prevention and therapy of work-related illnesses. More than 55,000 visitors and more than 1,600 exhibitors.

MEDICA with Compamed
November • Düsseldorf, Germany • **medica.de** • **compamed-tradefair.com** Considered the world's most important and largest international fair for medical equipment. Medica attracts 147,000 trade visitors from more than 70 countries and over 4,500 exhibitors from 80 countries. Compamed, the marketplace for suppliers to the medical manufacturing industry, attracts 600 exhibitors from 40 countries.

FIBO
April • Cologne, Germany • **fibo.de** The world's leading trade show for fitness, wellness and health. More than 80,000 visitors from 100 countries and more than 650 exhibitors from 38 countries.

OTWorld
May • Leipzig, Germany • **ot-leipzig.de** Innovative technology, new products and high quality professional training. The orthopedic and rehabilitation industry's leading event worldwide. More than 19,500 international visitors and 537 exhibitors.

IDS (International Dental Show)
March • Cologne, Germany • **english.ids-cologne.de** The world's leading trade show for the dental industry, including dental practices, dental labs and the specialist dental trade. More than 125,000 visitors from 150 countries; more than 2,000 exhibitors from 56 countries.

Additional Market Research
Links are provided as a convenience and for informational purposes only; they do not constitute an endorsement or an approval by the Department of Commerce of any product, service or opinion of any organization or individual. The Department of Commerce bears no responsibility for the accuracy, legality or content of external sites or for that of listed links. Contact the external site for answers to questions regarding its content.

BVMED Annual Report (2014–15)
https://www.bvmed.de/print/de/bvmed/publikationen/jahresberichte/bvmed-annual-report-2015

Ernst & Young Medical and Biotech Reports
http://www.ey.com/GL/en/Industries/Life-Sciences

This Page Intentionally Left Blank

Japan

Japan's market for medical devices and materials continues to be among the world's largest. According to the latest official figures from the Ministry of Health, Labor and Welfare (MHLW) Annual Pharmaceutical Production Statistics, the Japanese market for medical devices and materials in 2013 was approximately $33.6 billion (up 3.2 percent from 2012 in yen terms). Japan's total imports of U.S. medical devices were approximately $7.7 billion in 2013. In the near-term, the market is expected to increase due to Japan's aging population and continued demands for advanced medical technologies.

Overall Rank

2

The market remains heavily dependent on imports, especially for sophisticated medical technologies. U.S. exports to Japan have a 23 percent total market share, according to the official figures. For advanced devices and diagnostics, however, the total market share of U.S.-origin medical devices in Japan would be significantly higher than suggested by official statistics, approaching 60 percent for advanced medical technologies. U.S. medical device companies produce a wide variety of medical devices, but they are especially strong in sophisticated segments of the market, such as pacemakers, advanced interventional cardiology products, orthopedic implants, laser surgical equipment and advanced diagnostic imaging equipment. In the near-term, the market is expected to increase in a measured fashion. Japan's aging population, continued demand for advanced medical technologies and the Government of Japan's measures to promote the healthcare industry will sustain growth.

Market Entry

Japan does not levy customs duties on medical devices. Medical devices are heavily regulated under the Pharmaceutical and Medical Device Law (PMDL or PMD Act.). The Pharmaceutical Affairs Law (PAL) was amended and renamed the PMDL on November 25, 2014. The PMDL will enable further improvements to the regulatory review process, including the establishment of a device-specific regulatory framework. Notable changes under the PMDL include expanding the scope of products eligible for third-party certification; allowing quality inspections to be conducted for product groupings, as opposed to individual products; simplifying the

Country Highlights
Capital: Tokyo
Population: 127,064,340 (2014)
GDP: $4.901 trillion (2014)
Currency: Yen (JPY/¥)
Language: Japanese
Contact: Hiroyuki Hanawa, Senior Commercial Specialist
hiroyuki.hanawa@trade.gov
+81-3-3224-5083

manufacturer accreditation process; and making stand alone software a Class II device.

A Japanese company that intends to market a U.S. medical device needs to receive a "license for manufacturing/marketing business" (seizo hanbai gyo kyoka). The company holding this license is called a "Marketing Authorization Holder (MAH)." An MAH must be physically located in Japan. The MAH must obtain marketing approval (hanbai shonin) for each product. A U.S. manufacturer intending to manufacture medical devices in the United States and export them to Japan is required to be registered by the Pharmaceutical and Medical Device Agency (PMDA) as a "Registered Foreign Manufacturer" in a manner similar to that with which a Japanese manufacturer is registered. Typically, an MAH can make a registration application on behalf of a U.S. manufacturer. A U.S. manufacturer that lacks a Japanese subsidiary can receive and maintain the marketing approval under its own name. The U.S. company, however, will need to designate an MAH when applying for product approval. This Designated MAH (D-MAH) will have to assume the same responsibilities as an MAH. A D-MAH can be a regulatory consulting company or an importer/distributor that holds an MAH license. When a regulatory consultant is designated as an MAH, a U.S. company will need to have a Japanese distribution partner since a regulatory consulting company will not act as a distributor. If a U.S. company has a subsidiary in Japan, that subsidiary can become an MAH and then obtain the marketing approval for each product. If a U.S. company does not have a subsidiary in Japan, the company has three options to consider in order to conduct business in Japan:

- The U.S. company can ask their importer/distributor to obtain the marketing approval under the name of the importer/distributor. In this case, the importer/distributor will have complete control of the U.S. company's products when the products are marketed in Japan.
- The U.S. company can obtain the marketing approval under their own name by designating their importer/distributor as a D-MAH.
- The U.S. company can obtain the marketing approval under their own name via a neutral third party, such as a regulatory consulting company that has a "license for manufacturing/marketing business," by designating them as a D-MAH.

Current Market Trends

The Japanese market for medical devices is large and established, reaching $33.3 billion in 2013. The official figures for U.S. exports to Japan were limited to a 23 percent market share; however, according to the American Medical Devices and Diagnostics Manufacturers' Association (AMDD), an industry organization that represents the Japanese operations of 67 U.S.-based companies, approximately 60 percent of "new medical devices" approved in Japan were from AMDD member companies. Espicom Business Intelligence estimated that Japan's medical device market will exhibit a compound annual growth rate (CAGR) of 3.8 percent from 2013 to 2018, and the company estimated that all individual product categories should experience positive growth with the top performers being orthopedics and prosthetics (4.7 percent CAGR in local currency terms) and diagnostic imaging (3.9 percent).

Japan has a fast-aging demographic profile, with relatively prosperous seniors holding increasing expectations for improved quality of life in their later years. The Japanese health care system places increasing emphasis on improved treatment and health maintenance. This will generate further opportunity for the types of innovative solutions at which U.S. industry excels. In addition to sophisticated new medical devices, regenerative medicine and Health IT are subsectors that are particularly suited to meeting Japan's healthcare needs in the long run.

In November 2014, the PAL was amended and renamed to the Pharmaceutical and Medical Devices Law (PMDL). The PMDL will enable further improvements to the regulatory review process, including the establishment of a new product category for regenerative medicine products. Regenerative medicine is a branch of medical research in tissue engineering and molecular biology which deals with replacing, engineering or regenerating human cells, tissues or organs to restore or establish normal function. The rapid approval system on regenerative medical products was introduced with the enforcement of the law, which raised Japan to the forefront of regenerative medicine. The Ministry of Economy, Trade and Industry (METI) released a research report on the market of regenerative medicine and related peripheral industries in February 2013: total market size of the clinical regenerative market in 2012 was estimated as 9.1 billion yen ($86.0 million at the rate of 105.74 yen to the dollar), which was about one-eighth of the U.S. market. METI's report projected that Japan's regenerative medicine market would grow in 2020 to 95.4 billion yen ($902.2 million) and to 10.31 trillion yen ($9.75 billion) in 2030, roughly one-quarter of the U.S. market. METI also projected that the peripheral business, such as cell culture and processing facilities, devices, reagents, logistics and other contract services, was 17 billion yen ($160.7 million) in 2012, 95 billion yen ($898.4 million) in 2020 and 550 billion yen ($5.2 billion) in 2030.

Health IT: Japan ranked in the top position among 80 countries according to country case studies on healthcare IT metrics by the International Trade Administration of the U.S. Department of Commerce. For one such metric, Japan has the third highest GDP level globally (behind only the United States and China); a large Health IT market size (exceeding $1 billion); the oldest-skewing population distribution; a high concentration of population clustered in urban areas; a tech-friendly society; and very good Health IT infrastructure. All of these factors indicate that Health IT already has a good foundation in Japan, with the potential for more growth.

Main Competitors

The major product categories comprising Japan's domestic medical device production include: diagnostic imaging equipment; therapeutic and surgical equipment; biophenomena measuring and monitoring systems, home therapeutic equipment, dialyzers, and endoscopes. Japanese medical device companies maintain high market share in those product segments. Top Japanese medical device companies, in terms of sales, include Terumo®, NIPRO®, Olympus Medical Systems®, Toshiba Medical Systems®, Hitachi Medico®, Nihon Koden®, and Fukuda Denshi®. U.S. medical device companies produce a wide variety of medical devices, but they are especially strong in sophisticated segments of the medical market such as pacemakers, advanced interventional cardiology products, orthopedic implants, laser surgical equipment, and advanced diagnostic imaging equipment. Most major U.S. and foreign medical device companies have either a Japan office or a Japanese partner. As such, new-to-market U.S. companies will face strong competition not only from Japanese companies but also from U.S. and multinational companies already in the market. In April 2009, Japan based U.S. medical device manufacturers launched a new association called the American Medical Devices and Diagnostics Manufacturers Association (AMDD, *amdd.jp/en*). The AMDD currently has more than 65 member companies.

Current Demand

Given Japan's aging population and the increasing number of patients with chronic and life-style diseases, medical devices that alleviate pain, complement lost functions and improve the quality of life should show steady growth in demand. Also, the markets for in-home care devices, technologies and health IT related products are expected to grow as the number of people in out-patient care increases. Due to stronger consumer health concerns, other promising growth areas include self-care and preventive care medical devices and products.

Registration Process

Japan's medical device classification system is based on the Japanese Medical Device Nomenclature (JMDN) codes, which are different from U.S. and European classifications. The review processes for medical devices differ depending on the classification. Medical devices are classified by risk level into four classes (Class 1, Class 2, Class 3 and Class 4). Class 1 (lowest risk) is defined as general medical devices; Class 2 (relatively low risk) is defined as controlled medical devices; Class 3 (relatively high risk) and Class 4 (highest risk) are defined as specifically controlled devices. General medical devices can be marketed by submitting a notification to the Pharmaceutical and Medical Device Agency (PMDA). Controlled medical devices, with established certification standards, can be reviewed by third-party certification bodies. Controlled medical devices without certification standards and specifically controlled devices must be reviewed by PMDA and approved by MHLW.

Barriers

While the regulatory environment is expected to continue improving and the market for U.S. medical equipment in Japan remains strong, U.S. companies face challenges with pricing and reimbursement due to the Government of Japan's efforts to contain overall healthcare costs as a result of Japan's aging population. In the short-term, the postponing of scheduled tax hikes from 8 percent in October 2015 to 10 percent in April 2017 has created a more challenging financial environment as it generates additional revenues to fund healthcare expenditure. Price revisions and the lowering of reimbursement rates for three years in succession from 2016–18 have put pressure on medical device manufacturers to meet these fiscal restraints. Should potential price revisions under the proposed 2017 consumption tax raise take place, and the scheduled biennial price revisions occur in even-numbered fiscal years (2016 and 2018), this will lead to de facto annual revisions. Both U.S. and Japanese pharmaceutical industries are concerned that these changes could be used by advocates as ammunition to push for their proposal for annual revisions to continue from 2019.

Trade Events

MEDICAL Japan
February • Osaka, Japan • **medical-jpn.jp/en**
Bio Asia International Conference
March • Tokyo, Japan • **10times.com/bio-asia-international**

International Technical Exhibition of Medical Imaging (ITEM)
April • Yokohama, Japan • **jira-net.or.jp/e** A comprehensive academic exhibition for the latest medical imaging systems and peripheral devices.

CPhI Japan
April • Tokyo, Japan • **cphi.com/japan**

MEDTEC Japan
April • Tokyo, Japan • **medtecjapan.com/en**

BIOtech Japan
May • Tokyo, Japan • **bio-t.jp/en**

INTERPHEX Japan
June • Tokyo, Japan • **interphex.jp/en**
International Modern Hospital Show (IMHS)
July • Tokyo, Japan

CEATEC Japan
October • Tokyo, Japan • **www.ceatec.com/en**

HOSPEX Japan (International Hospital Engineering Exhibition)
November • Tokyo, Japan • **www.jma.or.jp/hospex/en**

Canada

The Canadian medical device market was valued at approximately $8 billion in 2014, making it the ninth largest market in the world. Canada's medical device imports totaled approximately $6.3 billion in 2014. The United States is the biggest exporter of medical devices to Canada, accounting for approximately 45 percent of imports or nearly $3 billion.

Overall Rank

4

Canada's healthcare industry depends heavily on the demand created by the country's publicly funded and insured health care system. The medical device industry consists of companies that produce a wide range of products used for diagnosis and treatment of ailments, which include the following: medical, surgical and dental equipment (including electro-medical equipment and related software), furniture, supplies and consumables, orthopedic appliances, prosthetics and diagnostic kits, reagents, and equipment.

The Canadian healthcare system falls under the jurisdiction of each province and territory. While funding is subsidized through federal transfer payments, the delivery and management of healthcare services are controlled by the provincial governments. Healthcare systems in Canada use various competitive tendering processes for the procurement of medical devices and diagnostics technologies. These change depending on the province but are generally conducted by each hospital and depend on the need and resources available to the hospital.

Imported products constitute 80 percent of the Canadian medical device market. There is particular demand for diagnostic equipment, as well as consumables, patient aids, orthopedic and prosthetic equipment, and dental equipment. The orthopedic and prosthetic equipment subsector is experiencing the strongest growth. The three largest provincial markets in the country are Ontario, Quebec and British Columbia. There are nearly 1,500 manufacturers of medical devices in Canada, employing approximately 35,000 people across the country.

Country Highlights
Capital: Ottawa
Population: 35.75 million (est. 2015)
GDP (USD): 1.785 trillion (est. 2014)
Currency: Canadian Dollar (CAD)
Language: English, French
Contact: Connie Irrera, Commercial Specialist
connie.irrera@trade.gov

Medical device manufacturers should develop partnerships with Canadian distributors to sell their products. To do this, they must obtain an establishment license and, if necessary, a device license. Imported medical devices are subject to Canadian safety and effectiveness regulations and packaging requirements. Few other barriers exist for U.S. companies looking to sell in Canada.

Market Entry

Health Canada, under the authority of the Food and Drugs Act, regulates the sale of medical devices in Canada. Health Canada is the equivalent regulatory agency to the U.S. Food and Drug Administration (FDA). Medical equipment imports must comply with marking, labeling and packaging requirements as described in the Food and Drug Act. In particular, instructions (operator's manual) accompanying the equipment must be in both of Canada's official languages (English and French).

Current Market Trends

Hospitals and other public health institutions are the principal purchasers of medical equipment and supplies, accounting for about 70 percent of total market demand in Canada. These organizations buy directly from manufacturers for capital equipment and use group procurement and distribution for regular medical equipment, including devices, instruments and supplies.

The demand for diagnostic equipment accounted for approximately 12 percent of the total medical devices imports in 2014, which includes technologies such as nuclear medicine cameras, MRI (magnetic resonance imaging) and CT (computed tomography). Other medical electro-diagnostic and patient monitoring equipment, including ultraviolet or infrared rays and ultrasonic scanners, will also see an increased demand. Other top contributors to the medical device import market in 2014 were instruments and appliances (8.3 percent), bougies, catheters, drains, sondes, and parts (3 percent), and artificial parts of the body (1.7 percent).

Main Competitors

The United States is by far the biggest exporter of medical devices to Canada, accounting for approximately 45 percent of the country's medical device imports. Other key import sources include Switzerland (13 percent), Germany (8.6 percent) and the United Kingdom (5.3 percent).

Current Demand

The Canadian medical device market depends upon imports for about 80 percent of its consumption. The import market is expected to grow at a 4.4 annual percent rate through 2016. Orthopedic and prosthetic equipment imports are projected to expand at a growth rate of 8.3 percent, while demand for all other medical device categories is expected to grow by at least 3 percent per year.

Canada's elderly population continues to grow: 15.7 percent of the population is aged 65 and over, and this demographic is expected to increase to 18.2 percent by 2016. This rapid aging of the population presents a key market opportunity for companies in the medical device industry.

Registration Process

Canadian authorities have worked at harmonizing regulations with those of the United States and Europe. In keeping with international trends, medical devices are regulated under the Food and Drugs Act as Class I (low risk), II, III or IV (high risk) devices, subject to Health Canada approval. All medical devices require an establishment license, and Class II, III and IV devices require a device license. All products are subject to safety and effectiveness requirements, including Class I devices, and these requirements must be satisfied with objective, documented evidence.

Barriers

Canada's population is largely along its southern border with the United States, and many areas are geographically remote and therefore difficult to access. The Canadian economy is threatened by debt and a decline in oil revenues and a need to reduce budget deficits, which may limit provincial spending. Furthermore, there is a lack of health policy cohesion between provinces and the potential for provincial healthcare spending cuts and a record of under-investment in medical technology. Economists report market barriers in the form of a potential slowdown in market and import growth and currency weakness hindering import growth.

Trade in the medical device market presents a number of advantages to U.S. companies. U.S. companies benefit from similarities between U.S. and Canadian regulations concerning the safety and quality of medical devices. Other advantages include the similarity between general business practices, the established reputation of U.S. companies in Canada and the close geographic proximity to Canada. Partnerships with the provincial and territorial health authorities responsible for the delivery of health care services are essential for the importing success of medical devices.

Trade Events

HealthAchieve
November • Toronto, Canada • *healthachieve.com*
The largest health care gathering in Canada.
Conference program with educational sessions;
exhibition floor hosting 350 exhibitors showcasing
health care products, services and technologies.
Approximately 9,000 delegates annually.

Resources

Health Canada, *hc-sc.gc.ca*

Statistics Canada, *statcan.gc.ca*

Healthcare Procurement
MERX—Canadian Public Tenders, *merx.com*
SEAO—Official Tendering Site of the Government of
Québec, *seao.ca*

Government Health Plans (by Province)

Alberta—Alberta Health, *health.alberta.ca*
British Columbia—B.C. Health,
www2.gov.bc.ca/gov/content/health

Manitoba—Manitoba Health, Healthy Living and
Seniors, *gov.mb.ca/health*

New Brunswick—New Brunswick Health,
bit.ly/1Ijh1w4

Newfoundland and Labrador—Department of Health
and Community Services, *health.gov.nl.ca*

Northwest Territories—Health and Social Services,
www.hss.gov.nt.ca

Nova Scotia—Nova Scotia Department of Wellness,
novascotia.ca/dhw

Nunavut—Department of Health, *gov.nu.ca/health*

Ontario—Ministry of Health and Long-Term Care,
health.gov.on.ca

Prince Edward Island—Health PEI, *healthpei.ca*

Québec—Régie de l'Assurance Maladie du Québec,
www.ramq.gouv.qc.ca/en

Saskatchewan—eHealth Saskatchewan,
ehealthsask.ca

Yukon—Health and Social Services, *hss.gov.yk.ca*

This Page Intentionally Left Blank

Australia

The Australian medical equipment industry sector has consistently provided good prospects for U.S. exporters. Australia is the eighth largest market for U.S. exporters of medical products. Approximately 80 percent of medical devices and diagnostics used in the market are imports. The three major suppliers are the United States, the European Union and Japan. U.S. medical equipment is traditionally well received due to its perceived high quality. The market is sophisticated, mature, and quick to adopt new healthcare technologies. Importers seek to obtain cost-effective and innovative products that will improve patient outcomes and reduce healthcare costs.

Overall Rank

10

Market Entry

Successful market entry strategies for Australia have three common elements: understanding the market, selecting the optimal partner and providing ongoing support to that partner. It is important to gain an understanding of the Australian context for a product or service, its competitors, standards, regulations, sales channels and applications. Success in the market will require appointing an Australian distributor or establishing a local subsidiary and setting up a local sales presence. Typically, distributors for medical products will cover the entire country and some may also have a subsidiary office in New Zealand. Given the size of the Australian continent—the same size as continental United States—and the distance from other countries, local support and service is important. Most of the criteria U.S. companies use to select distributors are applicable to Australia, with expectations adjusted to the scale of the market given the population of 23.8 million. Performing due diligence on potential local partners is just as important as in the United States.

Current Market Trends

Australia has a high per capita income, and there is demand for a full range of medical equipment. The $5 billion market is price sensitive and competitive. Australia spends approximately 9.7 percent of its GDP on healthcare, which is similar to the United Kingdom but less than the United States. Australia's aging population will significantly influence the demand for products and products that serve the aging population are likely to experience growth.

Country Highlights
Capital: Canberra
Population: 23.8 million
GDP (USD): 1.525 trillion
Currency: Australian Dollar (AUD)
Language: English
Contact: Monique Roos,
Commercial Specialist
monique.roos@trade.gov
+61-2-9373-9210
(514) 908-3662

The growth of chronic disease in Australia is similar to that in other developed nations. Australians increasingly suffer from asthma; cancer; diabetes; obesity; heart, stroke, and vascular disease; osteoarthritis, rheumatoid arthritis; and osteoporosis. Opportunities exist for technologies that avert or reduce disability because of these diseases.

Main Competitors

Imports supply approximately 80 percent of Australia's demand for medical equipment. Key suppliers include the United States, the European Union, Switzerland and Japan. Many suppliers in the Australian industry are subsidiaries of overseas corporations. The major U.S. medical companies represented in Australia (either through local representatives or subsidiary offices) include: 3M®, Bard®, Baxter Healthcare®, Becton Dickinson, ® Boston Scientific, ® Cook Medical, ® Johnson & Johnson Medical, ® Medtronic, ® St. Jude Medical, ® Stryker ® and Zimmer®. U.S. companies may experience strong competition from other U.S. companies or multinationals already in the market.

Current Demand

Australia's high standard of medical practice and aging population underpin a continued demand for a range of sophisticated, high quality and innovative medical equipment. Importers seek to source cost-effective and innovative products that will improve patient outcomes and reduce healthcare costs. Opportunities exist for products that provide a significant improvement in clinical outcomes and products with clearly differentiated capabilities. There is also a growing demand for products that lead to faster patient recovery, reduce hospital and rehabilitation costs and alleviate or manage disability and chronic pain.

Both the public and private sectors provide healthcare in Australia; as a result, government healthcare policies and public health influence the volume and pricing of healthcare products and services. Federal and State government spending accounts for 70 percent of total healthcare expenditure. The non-governmental sector (individuals and private health insurance) funds are the remaining 30 percent. Approximately 45 percent of Australians have private health insurance.

Registration Process

The Therapeutic Goods Administration (TGA) regulates the medical equipment industry.

Australia's regulatory framework is based on Global Harmonization Task Force (GHTF) and European Community guidelines. U.S. exporters must appoint an Australian representative/ sponsor to obtain regulatory approval from the TGA. U.S.-manufactured medical devices require an EC Certificate from a European Union Notified Body. Alternatively, U.S. manufacturers can apply to the TGA for a Conformity Assessment Certificate. Further information is available at *tga.gov.au*.

Trade Events

AusBiotech
October • Melbourne, Victoria • *ausbiotechnc.org*

Resources

Australian Government Department of Health, *health.gov.au*

NSW Health, *tenders.nsw.gov.au/health*

Health Purchasing Victoria, *hpv.org.au*

Queensland Health, *health.qld.gov.au*

Department of Human Services, *humanservices.gov.au*

Mexico

Mexico is a sizeable market for all types of medical devices. Imports of equipment, instruments, disposable and dental products reached $4.1 billion in 2014. Imports of U.S. products are duty free if they comply with the NAFTA certificate of origin. U.S. products are valued because of their high quality, after sales service and good prices compared to competing products. U.S. companies should take advantage of geographical proximity to start or grow their presence in Mexico.

Overall Rank

11

Market Entry

All medical equipment and devices can be imported duty free with a NAFTA certificate of origin. Imports are subject to a 16 percent VAT tax. All medical and health care products that touch or affect the human body must be registered with the Mexican Secretariat of Health (SSA) prior to sale or use in Mexico. Foreign manufacturers need a legally appointed Mexican distributor/ representative, who will be in charge of obtaining the sanitary registration/ market approval and will be the responsible for the product(s) in Mexico. The Commercial Service in Mexico can provide a detailed list of requirements and advice for processing market approval in that country for U.S. medical devices.

Current Market Trends

Most large public and private hospitals desire modern and very specialized medical devices. Some medium and small private hospitals with limited budgets buy used or refurbished equipment. Public hospitals by law cannot buy used or refurbished products. In order to save resources, recently, many public and private hospitals have been hiring companies that offer "integral surgery services" and provide service "per event," offering all the necessary products required to perform a surgery. This concept has been expanded to other areas where hospitals can use integral suppliers for different processes, like sterilization. In this way, hospitals avoid making large investments in materials, pharmaceuticals and instruments and also reduce the costs involved in keeping and controlling inventories and maintaining instruments for specialized surgeries.

Country Highlights
Capital: Mexico City
Population: 120 million (est. 2013)
GDP (USD): 1.26 trillion (2014)
Currency: Mexican peso (MXN)
Language: Spanish
Contact: Alicia Herrera, Senior Commercial Specialist
alicia.herrera@trade.gov
(011-52-55) 5140-2629

All public institutions ask suppliers to register with their organization. These institutions may award purchases under $3,100 directly to a selected provider. Purchases over that amount must be done through public tenders. All private health care facilities select suppliers by requesting price quotations. Their decisions are based on the best equipment at the best price.

Main Competitors

Most large international corporations offering medical devices have a presence in Mexico. Medium and small foreign suppliers usually sell through legally appointed distributors.

Current Demand

Public health care institutions account for 70 to 80 percent of total medical services provided nationwide while private health care institutions cover approximately 25 to 30 percent of the Mexican population, including 32 million people with private medical and accident insurance. Some patients affiliated with social security also have private medical insurance.

In the public sector, there are 1,169 hospitals, 194 of which are highly specialized medical units. In the private sector of 3,560 hospitals, only about 100 have over 50 beds and offer highly specialized medicine. Most of the hospitals offering specialty health care services are located in medium and large Mexican cities. There are also some medium sized private hospitals that offer specialty services and focus on high income, insured patients.

Imports supply about 80 percent of medical equipment and instruments and about 40 percent of medical disposable and dental products. In 2014, total imports in these four groups of products reached $4.1 billion. Of these imports, 55 percent, or $2.3 billion dollars, were of U.S. origin. Main competitors are from Belgium, Brazil, Canada, China, France, Germany, Israel, Italy, Japan, the Netherlands, South Korea and the United Kingdom.

Barriers

Obtaining sanitary registration and market approval of medical devices is often technical and time-consuming, but products that have been approved by the U.S. FDA generally are also approved in Mexico. Due to a shortage in resources, there have been some delays in receiving registration and marketing approvals from COFEPRIS, the Mexican Agency in charge or registering and approving medical devices, in the last two years.

COFEPRIS has worked closely with the industry to deregulate products that do not cause patient risk. On December 22, 2014, COFEPRIS published an agreement containing a list of 2,242 products that are no longer considered medical devices and, therefore, do not require sanitary registration/market approval in Mexico and can be freely imported. This list is to be updated periodically. COFEPRIS is also analyzing other ways to expedite the sanitary registration of FDA-approved medical devices.

To be imported into Mexico, some medical products need to comply with technical standards or NOMs (Norma Oficial Mexicana). Classification is based on the Harmonized System (HS).

There are few Mexican standards for medical devices, but various agencies are preparing more standards to be issued in the near future. Updated information on NOMs and other sanitary processes is available through COFEPRIS (***www.cofepris.gob.mx***).

Trade Events

AMIC Dental
November • Mexico City, Mexico • ***amicdental.com.mx***

Expomed
June • Mexico City, Mexico • ***expomed.com.mx***

Expo DICLAB
September 2016 • Mexico City, Mexico • ***expodiclab.com*** Clinical and scientific laboratory products.

Specialized events are also organized by medical academies and associations and may be excellent opportunities for companies offering high-technology medical devices.

Resources

Public Institutions
www.cofepris.gob.mx
www.salud.gob.mx
imss.gob.mx
www.issste.gob.mx
cenetec.salud.gob.mx
Private Hospitals
grupoempresarialangeles.com
hsj.com.mx
abchospital.com.mx
medicaltravel.com.mx
medicasur.com.mx

Additional Market Research
Links are provided as a convenience and for informational purposes only; they do not constitute an endorsement or an approval by the Department of Commerce of any product, service or opinion of any organization or individual. The Department of Commerce bears no responsibility for the accuracy, legality or content of external sites or for listed links. Contact the external site for answers to questions regarding its content.
COFEPRIS in English
http://www.cofepris.gob.mx/paginas/idiomas/ingles.aspx

Saudi Arabia

The Saudi health care sector is still the largest in the Near East North Africa region; the latest available figures indicate that the Saudi market for medical devices stood at $1.72 billion in 2013 and was expected to reach $1.88 billion in 2014 at more than 9 percent average annual growth. Imports account for more than 92 percent of the market at $1.59 billion, and U.S. companies command the list of suppliers with a 21 percent share of total imports.

Overall Rank

23

Healthcare and education remain a top priority for the Saudi government, representing about 44 percent of government spending. Budgeted expenditures for the healthcare and social affairs sectors in 2015 were set at $42.67 billion, a huge 48 percent growth from 2014 figures. Health care expenditures and delivery are dominated by the public sector, with government spending representing almost 79 percent of total spending on this sector, estimated at $20 billion annually.

Local manufacturing is still limited to consumables, including bandages, gloves, syringes and some furniture, including non-electrical beds.

Hospitals in Saudi Arabia are among the best equipped in this region, and the Ministry of Health sets aside an annual line item figure for "Replacement of Medical Equipment."

Market Entry

Although 100 percent foreign ownership of businesses in this sector is allowed, it is advisable that U.S. companies designate a local agent/representative to conduct business in Saudi Arabia. It is also advised that companies work with local legal counsel when drawing up a contractual agreement. Shari'a courts are the courts of general jurisdiction in the Saudi judicial system, and these courts review all foreign court decisions to ensure consistency with Shari'a law.

Medical equipment is charged a 5 percent customs duty; in some instances, however, imported equipment is exempted, notably if the shipment is bound for a government entity and/or a government project.

Country Highlights
Capital: Riyadh
Population: 29.9 million (est. 2014)
GDP (USD): 777.9 billion (2014)
Currency: Saudi riyal (SAR)
Language: Arabic (official)
Contact: Maher Siblini, Senior Commercial Specialist
maher.siblini@trade.gov
+966-11-488-3800 x4302
(514) 908-3662

Current Market Trends

Based on data from industry and the World Health Organization (WHO), Saudi Arabia, like other countries in the Arabian Gulf, continues to exhibit lifestyle change trends within its morbidity statistics. Non-communicable diseases, such as diabetes, cardiovascular diseases and cancer, have become the main causes of death and are estimated to account for 78 percent of total deaths. Additionally, the Kingdom has one of the world's highest rates of traffic accidents, which, in 2012, resulted in 5,200 deaths.

In turn, those figures have been the key drivers for various equipment and services, namely:

- emergency and trauma equipment,
- rehabilitation equipment,
- diagnostic equipment,
- electro-medical equipment,
- hospital beds,
- orthopedic appliances and prosthesis,
- dental equipment,
- laboratory equipment,

- hospital operation and management,
- e-Health, and
- generic pharmaceuticals.

Moreover, the Kingdom was recently hit by the Middle East Respiratory Syndrome (MERS) virus, resulting in 282 deaths. Lifestyle changes have created additional pressure on available resources and demand for the health care system, which, in general, suffers shortages in the number of physicians, nursing and technical staff.
WHO data revealed that 20 percent of nationals over the age of 20 suffered from type-2 diabetes, 35 percent of Saudi adults are obese and more than 6.5 percent of the population has high blood pressure.

As the public sector dominates the supply of health care services by accounting for the majority of health care expenditures, it represents approximately 79 percent of bed capacity. Industry sources expect the government sector to outpace the private sector in the level of investments and beds capacity. The latest figures suggest that the MoH bed capacity will almost double to 73,768 beds; the private sector will add 13,875 beds, raising its capacity to 26,000; and other government organizations will total 20,000 beds by 2020.

The Saudi government's 10th five year development plan (2015–19) stipulates:

- Improving emergency medical services
- Improving SFDA control and supervisory services
- Enhancing the application of cooperative health insurance
- Provide training and developing the skills of workforce
- Improving the performance efficiency of management and operation systems
- Improving healthcare services for the special-needs groups
- Reviewing the regulations related with medical malfunctions and violations
- Improving healthcare safety
- Encouraging health establishments to obtain international accreditation.
- Establishing more primary health care centers and specialized curative services
- Improving the quality of health services provided to children, the aged and the disabled and expanding home health care for the aged and disabled persons

- Increasing the role of the private sector in provision of health services and expanding the scope of medicines and medical appliances manufacturing
- Enhancing the e-health system and the supporting information systems and expanding the scope of their use
- Developing the preventive and curative health services provided to pilgrims and Omra performers and ensuring Haj seasons free of diseases and epidemics

Main Competitors

The Saudi market is extremely dependent on imports for medical devices. U.S. suppliers enjoy some advantages, including competitive prices, language and exchange rate. European suppliers are aggressively gaining market share with their close proximity to the market and perceived better customer support.

Current Demand

Total health care expenditures in 2015 are expected to remain at 2014 levels (at nearly $20 billion), due in part to lack of public funding for previous and ongoing projects, as well as the changes at the Ministry of Health administration (including a new minister). The demand for health care services has continuously outpaced supply, and both the public and private sectors are struggling to accommodate growing demand. A growing population, compulsory health insurance coverage and the prevalence of diseases are serving to boost the demand for services and hospital bed occupancy. Today, the overwhelming majority of Saudi Arabia's 8.5 million health insurance holders are expatriates. The insurance reform could swell the pool with more than 1 million Saudi civil servants plus about 5 million dependents.
New projects in the 2015 MoH budget included the construction of three hospitals, three blood bank centers, 11 primary health care centers and 10 comprehensive care clinics. Hospital beds currently exceed 64,000 for all hospitals in Saudi Arabia, and this figure is expected to grow to 119,000 beds by 2020. Moreover, a private group of investors is developing Riyadh's Medical Village over a 250,000 sq. m. area, which will consist of eight 130-bed hospitals, 60 outpatient clinics and other amenities and services.

Additionally, the Executive Board of the Health Ministers' Council for the GCC states (HO in Riyadh) release an annual tender valued for a couple of billions of dollars for:

- Hospital sundries
- Renal Dialysis supplies
- Oral and dental care
- Laboratory sundries
- Orthopedic and spinal surgery
- Rehabilitation
- Cardiovascular
- Linens and medical uniforms
- Ophthalmology sundries
- ENT sundries
- Medicines
- Vaccines
- Chemicals
- Insecticides
- Radio-pharmaceuticals
- Renal dialysis solutions

Major players in the Saudi health care sector include (by expenditures):

- Ministry of Health
- Saudi Arabian National Guard
- Ministry of Defense and Aviation
- Ministry of Higher Education
- General Organization for Social Insurance
- Ministry of Interior
- Royal Clinics
- Johns Hopkins Aramco Healthcare
- Private Sector
- GCC State Health Ministers Council Executive Board

Registration Process

The Saudi Food and Drug Authority (SFDA) monitors and controls the import and distribution of medical devices, pharmaceuticals and food products. For medical devices, the SFDA will usually accept, register and authorize the marketing and sale of any device that complies with applicable provisions of the SFDA's Interim Regulations and relevant regulatory requirements applicable in one or more of the countries of the Global Harmonization Task Force (GHTF), which includes Australia, Canada, Japan, U.S. and EU/EFTA. More information on the registration process can be found at *sfda.gov.sa/en*.

Barriers

Commercial Dispute Settlement

There is not yet a transparent, comprehensive legal framework in place for resolving commercial disputes. Saudi commercial law is still developing, but in 1994, the Saudis took the positive step of joining the New York Convention of 1958 on the Recognition and Enforcement of Foreign Arbitral Awards. Saudi Arabia is also a member of the International Center for the Settlement of Investment Disputes (also known as the Washington Convention). Dispute settlement in Saudi Arabia, however, continues to be time-consuming and uncertain. Even after a decision is reached in a dispute, effective enforcement of the judgment can still take years. Generally, the Board of Grievances has jurisdiction over disputes with the government and over commercial disputes.
In October 2007, King Abdullah issued a royal decree to overhaul the Kingdom's judicial system, including allocating SAR 7 billion (approximately $1.9 billion) to train judges and build new courts. The decree establishes two Supreme Courts, a general court, an administrative court and specialized labor and commercial tribunals, but implementation has been slow.

Business Visas

All visitors to Saudi Arabia must have a Saudi sponsor in order to obtain a business visa to enter Saudi Arabia. Business visitors and foreign investors can apply through the Saudi Arabian General Investment Authority (SAGIA) for a visitor visa at the Saudi Embassy or Consulates in the United States. Saudi Arabia has also begun to implement a decree stating that sponsorship for certain business visas is no longer required. Based on new instructions, the issuance of a visitor's visa should be affected within 24 hours from the application date.
While most business visas are valid for only one entry for a period of up to three months, the Saudi Embassy in Washington has begun issuing a five year multiple entry visa for selected business people, taking into consideration the principle of reciprocity. Finally, the Saudi Ministry of Foreign Affairs is currently examining the issuance of a visitor's visa at ports of entry for selected nationalities.

Delayed Payments

Payment delays are on the rise in the wake of lower oil prices, according to some members of the business community. Some companies carry Saudi government receivables for years before being paid. The government appears committed to clearing remaining arrears, but the problem persists. U.S. companies should check with the U.S. Embassy or Consulates if a problem arises.

Intellectual Property Protection

Saudi Arabia recently undertook a comprehensive revision of its laws covering intellectual property rights to bring them in line with the WTO agreement on Trade Related Aspects of Intellectual Property Rights (TRIPs). The Saudi legal system protects and facilitates acquisition and disposition of all property rights, including intellectual property. The Saudi government recently updated the Trademark Law (2002), the Copyright Law (2003) and the Patent Law (2004), with the dual goals of TRIPs compliance and effective deterrence against violators. In 2008, the Violations Review Committee created a website and has populated it with information on current cases. The government also endorsed the country's joining of the "Paris Convention for Protection of Industrial Property" and the "Berne Convention for the Protection of Literary and Artistic Works." Although intellectual property protection has steadily increased in the Kingdom, intellectual piracy remains a problem.

Arab League Boycott

The Gulf Cooperation Council (Saudi Arabia, Kuwait, Bahrain, Oman, Qatar and the United Arab Emirates) announced in the fall of 1994 that its members would no longer enforce the secondary and tertiary aspects of the Arab League Boycott. The primary boycott against Israeli companies and products still applies. Advice on boycott and anti-boycott related matters are available from the U.S. Embassy or from the Office of Anti-Boycott Compliance in Washington, D.C.

Government Procurement

Government contracts on project implementation and procurement strongly favor Saudi and GCC nationals. Most Saudi defense contracts, however, are negotiated outside these regulations on a case-by-case basis. Saudi Arabia published its revised government procurement procedures in August 2006. Foreign suppliers participating in government procurement are required to establish a training program for Saudi nationals. The Saudi Arabian government has yet to initiate accession procedures to join the WTO Government Procurement Agreement as agreed during the Kingdom's accession process. In addition, Saudi Arabia gives priority in government purchasing to GCC products. These items receive up to a 10 percent price preference over non-GCC products in all government procurements in which foreign suppliers participate.

Shipping

Saudi Arabia gives preference to national carriers for up to 40 percent of government-related cargos. Two local companies take full advantage of this situation. Standards and Labeling
As part of the GCC Customs Union, the six Member States are working toward unifying their standards and conformity assessment systems. Each Member State currently continues to apply its own standard or a GCC standard in this sector. A new ICCP mandates that a Certificate of Conformity must accompany all consumer goods exported to Saudi Arabia. Labeling and marking requirements are compulsory for any products exported to Saudi Arabia.

Trade Events

C3 Saudi International Healthcare Forum
April • Riyadh, Saudi Arabia Healthcare themes and issues. Drawing on high level officials and executives from both the public and privates sectors in the U.S. and Saudi Arabia.
Saudi Health Exhibition and Conference
May • Riyadh, Saudi Arabia Showcasing the latest products, technology and services. This is the only event with the full support of the Ministry of Health and will cover the full spectrum of healthcare.

Resources

Saudi Ministry of Health, *moh.gov.sa/en*
Executive Board of the Saudi Health Ministers Council, *sgh.org.sa/en-us/home.aspx*

Malaysia

Malaysia represents one of the more vigorous and vibrant medical device markets in Southeast Asia, presenting opportunities for U.S. exporters of medical technology to expand their sales into rising economies. Increasing patient access to healthcare will remain in the focus of the Government of Malaysia for the next five years, to include upgrading facilities and equipment, and expanding delivery systems.

Malaysia's national healthcare expenditure historically is around 4 to 5 percent of GDP. In 2014, the Malaysian government set aside approximately $5.83 billion, or 8.4 percent of the yearly national budget, for public healthcare. Out of this allocation, 7.5 percent is assigned for development purposes. Comparing public and private hospital expenditure, the public hospitals expenditure is about 65 percent while the private sector is around 35 percent. The number of hospital beds for both public and private healthcare combined has increased from 55,180 in 2010 to 58,530 in 2014. Public hospital beds accounted for 75 percent of total hospital beds in 2014.

Total two-way trade for Malaysia's medical device industry for 2014 is $1.98 billion. Malaysian imports of medical, surgical, dental and veterinary science instruments and devices amounted to $735 million. Singapore (27 percent) is the highest supplier to Malaysia. This is followed by the United States (19 percent), Germany (13 percent), Japan (8 percent), China (7 percent) and South Korea (3 percent). Overall, Malaysian medical device imports increased 8 percent over 2013. It is also worthwhile to note that Singapore is a major trans-shipment point for the Association of South East Asian Nations (ASEAN) region.

Exports for the same category of medical instruments and devices from Malaysia increased 24 percent to $1.24 billion in 2014. Top export destinations for Malaysia in this sector are the United States (43 percent), Germany (14 percent), Japan (22 percent) and Singapore (12 percent). It is also interesting to note a marked increase in total trade between Malaysia and the Netherlands. Total bilateral trade between Malaysia and Netherlands is

Country Highlights
Capital: Kuala Lumpur
Population: 29.9 million
GDP (USD): 326.93 billion (2014)
Currency: Ringgit Malaysia (MYR)
Language: Bahasa Malaysia
Contact: Tracy Yeoh, Commercial Specialist
tracy.yeoh@trade.gov
60-3-2168-5089

$60 million for 2014, a 143 percent increase since 2013.

The Government of Malaysia designated the Medical Device Industries sector as high growth potential in its next five year strategic economic plan (2016–20), also known as the 11th Malaysian Plan. According to the Malaysian Ministry of International Trade and Industry, from 2010 to 2014, foreign medical device industry investments into Malaysia totaled MYR 11 billion ($2.9 billion) while domestic investments were MYR 1.2 billion ($316 million).

Improving and achieving universal access to quality healthcare will be the focus of the Malaysian government for the next five years. The major thrusts will be in improving healthcare quality to underserved populations, as well as ensuring efficient and effective expansion of the healthcare delivery system. In addition to upgrading healthcare facilities, a government priority is to reduce communicable and non-communicable diseases (CD and NCD). E-Health Information and Communications Technology (ICT) strategy will be implemented concurrently to track and support these measures.

Market Entry

Many exporters designate a Malaysian-based trading company as their local sales agent responsible for handling customs clearance of imported goods, for dealing with established wholesalers and/or retailers, for marketing the product directly to major corporations or the government and for handling after-sales service. In some cases, especially when selling to the government, a Malaysian Bumiputra status distributor is required. The term Bumiputra refers to a Malaysian of Malay or indigenous racial origin.

The passing of Act 737 and Medical Device Regulations 2012 has changed the regulatory framework for Malaysia. Industry players intending to export to Malaysia now need to register their medical devices with the Malaysian Medical Device Authority. Pharmaceutical and health supplements registration is with the National Pharmaceutical Control Bureau.

Current Market Trends

Increasingly, more Malaysians are taking the approach of wellness and disease prevention rather than treatment. Food and vitamin supplements are seen as preventive measures towards maintaining optimal health. Basic vitamin and pro-vitamins, as well as natural and organic supplements, are gaining popularity. The United States is the largest supplier of healthcare supplements to Malaysia. U.S. brands are both trusted and well received by local consumers.

As for dental market trends, we are seeing subspecialties in the area of orthodontics, implant and esthetic procedures increasingly being offered in private dental clinics. The United States is one of the leading suppliers of orthodontics products in Malaysia.

Private healthcare services in Malaysia are predominantly used by the upper-middle to affluent segment of the population. As per capita GDP rises, demand for private healthcare consumption is expected to increase in tandem. Health screening is increasingly popular. Medical aesthetics procedures are also gaining ground in Malaysia.

Similar to other increasingly affluent countries, non-communicable diseases, such as diabetes, high-blood pressure, cardiovascular disease, oncology cases and obesity, are on the rise in Malaysia.

Main Competitors

The main competitors for U.S. companies in the Malaysian market are from the EU countries of Germany, the Netherlands, United Kingdom and France. Japan, China and South Korea have a strong presence in the Malaysian market as well. As noted above, statistical data show that the Netherlands made strong inroads into the Malaysian market in 2014 for the medical device sector with 143 percent total bilateral trade growth over 2013.

Current Demand

Consolidation is the key word for public healthcare resources and facilities. The Malaysian government is taking steps to implement a hospital cluster concept in select locations. Hospitals within a similar geographic region will serve as one unit sharing assets, amenities and human resources. Additionally, existing healthcare facilities and assets will also be upgraded. Healthcare services to the rural and remote areas will be expanded via mobile healthcare teams and flying doctor services.

Implementation of the e-Health strategy will include incorporating existing information and communications systems into one system-wide module. This should improve health data management and support research and development and commercialization initiatives.

Pre-hospital care, such as ambulance services and accidents/emergencies services, will also be a key focal area. Ideally, collaboration between private sector and non-governmental (NGO) ambulance service providers will improve response time and better resource utilization.

Demand for private healthcare has been increasing exponentially due to its speedy service delivery and quality healthcare. In 2013, private hospital outpatient attendance was 6.8 percent of overall outpatient care provided in-country. Private hospitals also command 32.2 percent of total hospital admissions. In 2013, approximately 25 percent of the doctors, 38 percent of dentists and 33 percent of pharmacists were in private practice.

Registration Process

The Malaysian Medical Device Act (Act 737) took effect in 2012. Related Regulations specify requirements and procedures to medical device registration, conformity assessment body (CAB) registration, establishment licensing, export permit and appeal.

The Regulations went into force on July 1, 2013. A transition period of two years for medical device registration and one year for establishment licensing was given to the industry before the Regulations were fully enforced. The Medical Device (Exemption) Order 2015 has extended the transition period of medical devices registration for another year, ending June 30, 2016.

Thereafter, all medical device manufacturers in Malaysia will need to register their medical devices with the Medical Device Authority. Importers and distributors will also need to obtain an establishment license to import and distribute medical devices locally in Malaysia.

Barriers

All foreign companies need to work with a Malaysian company that is registered with the Malaysian Ministry of Finance in order to bid for government tenders. Hence, most of the government tender information available online is in the local language, Bahasa Malaysia.

The Malaysian government is actively promoting local manufacturing of generic drugs and medical devices. There are instances of government procurement favoring locally produced and manufactured drugs, products and equipment—even when the bidding foreign companies' pricing is far lower, and the products and equipment are of equal or superior quality.

Trade Events

SE-Asian Healthcare Show
April • Kuala Lumpur, Malaysia • *abcex.com/usa* One of the region's most established trade shows, covering the entire healthcare industry. Regional visitors include Singapore, Indonesia and other neighboring countries.
APHM International Healthcare Conference
June • Kuala Lumpur, Malaysia • *aphmconferences.org* The Association of Private Hospitals of Malaysia (APHM) annual conference and exhibition. A significant annual medical event.

Resources

Healthcare Procurement, *moh.gov.my/english.php*
Government Health Plans, *rmk11.epu.gov.my/index.php/en*

This Page Intentionally Left Blank

Nigeria

The Nigerian healthcare sector is presently grossly underdeveloped and does not meet local needs. Much of the healthcare infrastructure is confined to major cities, with people living in urban areas getting four times as much access to healthcare as those living in the rural areas. The private health sector is highly fragmented, consisting of many small medical facilities that are privately owned by medical professionals. Most of these hospitals have few facilities and fewer than 10 beds.

Overall Rank

57

According to a 2015 BMI report, there were an estimated 3,534 hospitals in 2014, 950 of which were in the public sector. These included 54 federal tertiary hospitals comprising 20 teaching hospitals, 22 federal medical centers, three national orthopedic hospitals, the National Eye Centre, the National ENT Centre and 7 psychiatric hospitals, which are overseen by the Hospital Services Department of the Federal Ministry of Health (FMOH). The private sector is the dominant provider of care in many areas, accounting for the greater part of secondary care facilities. In 2005, the FMOH estimated that there were around 9,000 private health facilities, but information on their location and the level of care provided was patchy. Private health facilities are thought to include around 2,600 private hospitals and clinics. Nigeria had an estimated 134,000 hospital beds in 2014, equal to 0.8 per thousand populations, which is well below the rate for the African region. The number of hospital beds is estimated to have grown at a compound annual growth rate (CAGR) of 3.8 percent since 2009, slightly higher than population growth but at an insufficiently high rate to have a significant impact on the population bed ratio. The number of doctors is estimated to have grown at a CAGR of 2.7 percent since 2009, reaching 66,555 in 2014. The number of dentists is extremely low with less than 3,000 registered in 2014.

Despite these recent improvements, Nigeria's health infrastructure still remains low and insufficient to cater to the country's growing population. As a result, over 30,000 Nigerians travel to India, the United Arab Emirates, the United States, South Africa and Europe each year on medical tourism for major treatments, such as open heart surgeries, renal transplants, brain surgeries, cancer and eye treatment. An estimated $1 billion is spent on these

Country Highlights
Capital: Abuja
Population: 170,123,740 (est. 2012)
GDP (USD): 509 billion (2014)
Currency: Naira (NGN)
Language: English (official)
Contact: Chamberlain Eke, Commercial Specialist chamberlain.eke@trade.gov 234-1-460-3400 x3414

therapies. Nigeria's health sector contribution to GDP is 5 percent, and the country remains a net importer of medical equipment and prescription medicines. Local production of medical devices is limited to peripheral items, such as hospital beds and gurneys. Local pharmaceutical manufacturing companies only have the capacity to produce over-the-counter drugs, especially those for treating the common cold, malaria and headaches, as well as some low end prescription remedies. Prospects exist for U.S. companies largely in the medical diagnostics domain. Magnetic Resonance Imaging (MRI), Computed Tomography scanners (CT), Digital X-Ray, Ultrasound, Mammography, ultrasound scans, and anesthesia technologies will see demand.

In 2013, the Nigerian government announced a zero tariff on imported medical equipment, pharmaceutical manufacturing machinery and packaging materials, but industry sources say the legislation has not yet been implemented. A duty rate of 20 to 25 percent on medical equipment still applies.

Market Entry

As in many locations, the most effective way for U.S. manufacturers and suppliers to penetrate the Nigerian market is by taking advantage of the matchmaking services and programs of the Commercial Service in both the United States and Nigeria. For establishing a presence in Nigeria, we recommend that U.S. companies use agent/distributor relationships with local companies vetted by the Commercial Service in Nigeria. Contractual terms and conditions must be fully spelt out with local partners, and we recommend using the services of an attorney.

Current Market Trends

Consumer health has been gradually growing in the past 5 years due to increasing health awareness. Many Nigerians, however, still resort to self-medication rather than visit a hospital when in need of medical care, largely due to the relatively high cost of hospital treatment. About 61 percent of Nigerians live on less than $1 a day, according to country's statistics bureau, while 69 percent of health payments are out-of-pocket, according to the health ministry. The wealthy seek specialized care overseas because of the dearth of professional medical personnel and the dilapidated health infrastructure. Over the years, poor remuneration has forced many healthcare professionals to seek opportunities abroad, especially in Europe and the United States. The President of the Association of Nigerian Physicians in the Americas says the number of Nigerian doctors in the U.S. alone is between 4,000 and 5,000. Labor strikes by doctors employed both by federal and state hospitals are a regular feature. Thus, patients are often driven to seek medical attention from private clinics.

Despite these challenges, the Nigerian healthcare sector is expected to grow under the government's National Strategic Health Development Plan (NSHDP) introduced in 2010. Under the NSHDP, the Government of Nigeria and its institutional partners plan to spend $26.7 billion in the construction and upgrade of hospitals, diagnostic centers and laboratories; procurement of modern medical equipment and drugs; and manpower development.

Additionally, the Nigerian Health Insurance Scheme (NHIS), established in 2004 by the Nigerian government as its flagship affordable health insurance institution with the oversight to provide universal health coverage to its citizens, has licensed 60 Health Maintenance Organizations (HMOs). Although most of those enrolled into the NHIS program are public sector employees, private sector organizations and individuals are joining quickly. According to the NHIS, about 7.2 million Nigerians have so far been registered. The goal is to cover 100 percent of the population by 2020. This trend is expected to significantly increase the number of people with access to hospital care and reduce out-of-pocket payments.

A report published by Euromonitor International in May 2014 indicates that independent drug stores remain the major channels of distribution of consumer health products. Direct selling continues to be a relatively important sales method, which is partly responsible for driving overall growth of consumer health. Internet retailing, however, remains insignificant but is enjoying growth.

Main Competitors

According to industry intelligence, European products dominate the Nigerian market, but Chinese and Indian manufacturers have made significant inroads, especially in the low end medical devices segment. Asian manufacturers largely employ direct marketing methods and often travel to Nigeria to visit with suppliers and hospitals as part of their business development tactics.

Current Demand

Demand for diagnostic related equipment and technologies such as Magnetic Resonance Imaging (MRI), Computed Tomography scan (CT), Digital X-Ray, Ultrasound, Mammography, ultrasound scans, as well as anesthesia kits and mortuary equipment have increased significantly since the introduction of the National Strategic Health Development Plan (NSHDP). Used medical equipment is in high demand, especially by small and mid-sized private health clinics, diagnostic centers and laboratories due to their small budgets. Price and after sales support are the most competitive factors when selling to Nigeria.

Registration Process

The National Agency for Food and Drug Administration and Control (NAFDAC,

nafdac.gov.ng) regulates food and drug products in Nigeria.

For NAFDAC's guidelines on medical devices, visit *bit.ly/1D6zg7M*.

For guidelines on pharmaceutical products, visit *bit.ly/1JLLTCb*.

Due to the complications involved in the NAFDAC registration process, U.S. exporters are advised to encourage their Nigerian partners to seek registration on their behalf. A U.S. company does not need to re-register an already registered product with NAFDAC if it decides to change its local agent or distributor. In this case, the U.S. exporter simply needs to withdraw its power of attorney from its old local representative, give the power to its new partner and inform NAFDAC of the change in writing.

The Standard Organization of Nigeria (SON, *son.gov.ng*) is responsible for compliance with equipment specification and import standards. Importers of drug products and medical devices must first register them with NAFDAC prior to import.

Barriers

As stated above, in 2013, the Nigerian government announced a zero tariff on medical devices. To date, the new tariff regime still has not taken effect, leaving a duty rate of 20 to 25 percent.

Trade Events

Nigeria Pharma Manufacturers Expo
September • Lagos, Nigeria • *nigeriapharmaexpo.com*

Medic West Africa Exhibition and Congress
October • Lagos, Nigeria • *medicwestafrica.com*

Nigeria's healthcare professional associations include: the Nigerian Medical Association (NMA, *nigeriannma.org*), Association of General and Private Medical Practitioners of Nigeria (AGPMPN, *agpmpn.org*), Association of Medical Laboratory Scientists of Nigeria (AMLSN, *amlsn.org*), Pharmaceutical Society of Nigeria (PSN, *psnnational.org*), and Healthcare Federation of Nigeria (HFN).

This Page Intentionally Left Blank

Addendum: Resources for U.S. Exporters

The U.S. Government has numerous resources available to help U.S. exporters: from additional market research, to guides to export financing, to overseas trade missions, to staff around the country and the world. A few key resources are highlighted below. For additional information about services from the International Trade Administration (ITA), please visit www.export.gov.

Country Commercial Guides
http://export.gov/ccg/
Written by U.S. Embassy trade experts worldwide, the Country Commercial Guides provide an excellent starting point for what you need to know about exporting and doing business in a foreign market. The reports include sections addressing market overview, challenges, opportunities and entry strategies; political environment; selling U.S. products and services; trade regulations, customs, and standards; and much more.

Basic Guide to Exporting
http://export.gov/basicguide/
A Basic Guide to Exporting addresses virtually every issue a company looking to export might face. Numerous sections, charts, lists and definitions throughout the book's 19 chapters provide in-depth information and solid advice about the key activities and issues relevant to any prospective exporter.

Trade Finance Guide: A Quick Reference for U.S. Exporters
http://www.export.gov/tradefinanceguide/index.asp
Trade Finance Guide: A Quick Reference for U.S. Exporters is designed to help U.S. companies, especially small and medium-sized enterprises, learn the basics of trade finance so that they can turn their export opportunities into actual sales and achieve the ultimate goal of getting paid on time for those sales. Concise, two-page chapters offer the basics of numerous financing techniques, from open accounts to forfaiting and government assisted foreign-buyer financing.

Trade Missions
http://www.export.gov/trademissions/
Department of Commerce trade missions are overseas programs for U.S. firms that wish to explore and pursue export opportunities by meeting directly with potential clients in local markets. Trade missions include among other activities: one-on-one meetings with foreign industry executives and government officials that are pre-screened to match specific business objectives.

Certified Trade Fairs
http://www.export.gov/eac/show_short_trade_events.asp?CountryName=null&StateName=null&IndustryName=null&TypeName=International%20Trade%20Fair&StartDate=null&EndDate=null
The Department of Commerce's trade fair certification program endorses overseas trade shows that are a reliable venue and a good market for U.S. firms to sell their products and services abroad. These shows serve as a vital access vehicle for U.S. firms to enter and expand to foreign markets. The certified show/U.S. pavilion ensures a high-quality, multi-faceted opportunity for American companies to successfully market overseas. Among other benefits, certified trade fairs provide U.S. exhibitors with help facilitating contacts, market information, counseling, and other services to enhance their marketing efforts.

International Buyer Program
http://export.gov/ibp/
The International Buyer Program (IBP) brings thousands of international buyers to the United States for business-to-business matchmaking with U.S. firms exhibiting at major industry trade shows. Every year, the International Buyer Program results in millions of dollars in new business for U.S. companies by bringing pre-screened international buyers, representatives and distributors to selected shows. U.S. country and industry experts are on site at IBP shows to provide hands-on export counseling, market analysis, and matchmaking services. Each IBP show also has an International Business Center, where U.S. companies can meet privately with prospective international buyers, prospective sales representatives, and business partners and obtain assistance from experienced ITA staff.

The Advocacy Center
http://www.export.gov/advocacy/

The Advocacy Center coordinates U.S. government interagency advocacy efforts on behalf of U.S. exporters bidding on public-sector contracts with overseas governments and government agencies. The Advocacy Center helps to ensure that sales of U.S. products and services have the best possible chance competing abroad. Advocacy assistance is wide and varied but often involves companies that want the U.S. Government to communicate a message to foreign governments or government-owned corporations on behalf of their commercial interest, typically in a competitive bid contest.

U.S. Commercial Service
http://www.export.gov/usoffices/index.asp
With offices throughout the United States and in U.S. Embassies and consulates in nearly 80 countries, the U.S. Commercial Service utilizes its global network of trade professionals to connect U.S. companies with international buyers worldwide. Whether looking to make their first export sale or expand to additional international markets, companies will find the expertise they need to tap into lucrative opportunities and increase their bottom line. This includes trade counseling, actionable market intelligence, business matchmaking and commercial diplomacy.

The Global Healthcare Technologies Team
http://www.export.gov/industry/health/
The Global Healthcare Technologies Team is a specialized group within the U.S. Commercial Service that works to address issues and trade opportunities specific to the strong and growing healthcare sector, and to ensure you have the information you need to grow your business. The Global Healthcare Technologies Team is dedicated to enhancing the global competitiveness of the U.S. health industry,

expanding its market access, and increasing exports. It accomplishes this through a variety of resources and services for U.S. companies such as webinars, Gold Key and Platinum Key services. The team consists of trade specialists from throughout the U.S. and from U.S. Embassies around the world and provides market intelligence, business matchmaking, trade counseling, and regulations and customs navigation.

Discover Global Markets: Healthcare Connections - - Seattle, Washington, September 13-15, 2016
http://export.gov/discoverglobalmarkets/healthcare connections/
The *Discover Global Markets* series of international trade conferences has been a highly successful and unprecedented effort designed to help U.S. businesses expand sales, penetrate new markets, and boost their bottom line through exports. *Discover Global Markets: Healthcare Connections* is the must-attend event of the year for medical device companies. Featuring global updates on healthcare opportunities, regulations, and best practices for success, this conference will equip you to compete and win internationally. You will hear directly from industry leaders and connect with international buyers, network with healthcare companies from around the country and get breaking news on country market intelligence. *Discover Global Markets: Healthcare Connections* will feature panels on opportunities in the medical device sector, diagnostics, health IT, global health, and more. U.S. Embassy-based industry specialists from around the world will give updates on country projects and regulatory framework.

Appendix 1: Near-term Medical Device Export Market Rankings

1. Germany	31. Brazil
2. Japan	32. Turkey
3. Netherlands	33. Slovak Republic
4. Canada	34. Finland
5. Belgium	35. India
6. Switzerland	36. Spain
7. United Kingdom	37. Czech Republic
8. China	38. Hungary
9. France	39. Thailand
10. Australia	40. Russia
11. Mexico	41. Argentina
12. Austria	42. Kuwait
13. Norway	43. Colombia
14. Sweden	44. Portugal
15. Italy	45. South Africa
16. Korea	46. Oman
17. Denmark	47. Greece
18. Singapore	48. Jordan
19. Ireland	49. Bulgaria
20. Israel	50. Egypt
21. Taiwan	51. Romania
22. New Zealand	52. Ukraine
23. Saudi Arabia	53. Indonesia
24. Hong Kong	54. Philippines
25. United Arab Emirates	55. Morocco
26. Ghana	56. Kenya
27. Poland	57. Nigeria
28. Malaysia	
29. Chile	
30. Croatia	

Appendix 2: Questionnaire directed to ITA Global Health Team for individual country profiles

The Global Health Team, posted in U.S. Embassies and Consulates in more than 70 countries, was requested to supply updated market information. The Global Health Team investigates issues and trade opportunities specific to the strong and growing healthcare sector. To learn more about the ITA Global Health Team, please visit **export.gov/industry/health**.

The list of information requested from the Global Health Team is as follows:

Country Statistics
- Capital
- Population
- GDP
- Currency
- Language(s)

U.S. Commercial Service Contact Information
- Name
- Position
- Email
- Phone

Market Profile
- Executive Summary
- Market Entry
- Current Market Trends
- Main Competitors
- Current Demand
- Registration Process
- Barriers
- Trade Events
- Government Links
  - Healthcare Procurement
  - Government Health Plans

Appendix 3: Methodology

This study ranked U.S. export history heavily, as it would skew the next factor, R/R index, more strongly for a more "U.S.-centric" calculation. U.S. export history takes into account the issues that U.S. exporters currently face, including competition, market proximity and regulatory issues that affect their type of export (usually higher end). The R/R index is a very rich piece of data that involves a number of country and market risk and reward variables (*see* Appendix III below). To project into the future, this report uses a mixture of projected *per capita* and market size projections up to the year 2020. This report ranks *per capita* spending higher than size of market, as it would likely more adequately track with relatively more expensive U.S. exports.

Formula for Market Ranking
A.	U.S. Export History:	40%
B.	R/R Index:	35%
C.	Projected *per capita* health care spending:	20%
D.	Projected market size:	5%

Appendix 4: BMI Risk/Reward Index Methodology

BMI's Risk Reward Index (RRI) provides a comparative regional ranking system evaluating the ease of doing business and the industry-specific opportunities and limitations for potential investors in a given market.

The RRI system divides into two distinct areas:

Rewards:

This area consists of an evaluation of the sector's size and growth potential in each market and also broader industry/market characteristics that may inhibit its development. This is further broken down into two sub categories:

- Market Rewards: an industry specific category taking into account current industry size and growth forecasts, the openness of market to new entrants and foreign investors to provide an overall score for potential returns for investors

- Country Rewards: a country specific category whose score factors in favorable political and economic conditions for the industry

Risks:

This area consists of an evaluation of industry-specific dangers and those emanating from the market's political/economic profile that call into question the likelihood of anticipated returns being realized over the assessed time period. This is further broken down into two sub categories:

- Market Risks: an industry specific sub category whose score covers potential operational risks to investors, regulatory issues inhibiting the industry and the relative maturity of a market

- Country Risks: a country specific sub category in which political and economic instability, unfavorable legislation and a poor overall business environment are evaluated to provide an overall score

BMI makes its calculations taking a weighted average, combining market and country risks or market and country rewards. These two results in turn provide an overall RRI score, which is used to create a regional ranking system for the risks and rewards of involvement in a specific industry in a particular country.

For each category and sub-category, each market is scored out of 100 (100 being the best), with the overall RRI a weighted average of the total score. Importantly, as most of the countries and territories evaluated are considered by BMI to be Emerging Markets, the index is revised on a quarterly basis. This ensures that the index draws on the latest information and data across our broad range of sources and the expertise of our analysts.

BMI's approach in assessing the risk/reward balance for industry investors globally is fourfold:

- First, BMI identifies factors (in terms of current industry/country trends and forecast industry/country growth) that represent opportunities to would-be investors.

- Second, BMI identifies country and industry-specific traits that pose or could pose operational risks to would-be investors.

- Third, BMI attempts, where possible, to identify objective indicators that may serve as proxies for issues/trends to avoid subjectivity.

- Finally, BMI uses its proprietary Country Risk Index (CRR) in a nuanced manner to ensure that only the aspects most relevant to the infrastructure industry are incorporated. Overall, the system offers an industry-leading, comparative insight into the opportunities/risks for companies across the globe.

Appendix 5: Citations

[1] HTS codes used for forecasting and trade calculations: 300510, 300590, 300610, 300640, 300650, 300680, 300691, 300692, 340700, 401511, 401519, 420600, 420610, 611510, 611512, 611519, 611592, 611593, 630720, 630790, 650610, 681250, 681280, 681291, 841920, 841990, 854370, 854380, 854389, 871310, 871390, 871420, 901811, 901812, 901813, 901814, 901819, 901820, 901831, 901832, 901839, 901841, 901849, 901850, 901890, 901910, 901920, 902000, 902110, 902111, 902119, 902121, 902129, 902130, 902131, 902139, 902140, 902150, 902190, 902211, 902212, 902213, 902214, 902219, 902221, 902229, 902230, 902290, 902511, 902519, 940210, 981000, 382100, 382200.

[2] *The State of the U.S. Medtech Industry,* January 2015, Anchin, Block & Anchin

[3] *The State of the U.S. Medtech Industry,* January 2015, Anchin, Block & Anchin, LLP available at http://www.anchin.com/admin/Upload/Document/MDDI_2015-01_LS.pdf.

[4] *The U.S. Medical Device Industry,* Made in America Movement at www.themadeinamericamovement.com/reshoring/u-s-medical-device-industry/ sourced from Expansion Solutions Magazine, by SelectUSA at http://www.expansionsolutionsmagazine.com/industry_articles/view/9210/the_u_s__medical_device_industry]

Industry & Analysis' (I&A) staff of industry, trade and economic analysts devise and implement international trade, investment, and export promotion strategies that strengthen the global competitiveness of U.S. industries. These initiatives unlock export, and investment opportunities for U.S. businesses by combining in-depth quantitative and qualitative analysis with ITA's industry relationships.

For more information, visit
www.trade.gov/industry

I&A is part of the International Trade Administration, Whose mission is to create prosperity by strengthening the competitiveness of U.S. industry, promoting trade and investment, and ensuring fair trade and compliance with trade laws and agreements.

INTERNATIONAL
TRADE
ADMINISTRATION

www.ingramcontent.com/pod-product-compliance
Lightning Source LLC
Chambersburg PA
CBHW081750280526
45789CB00008B/2811